Doe,
   Ray,
      Me

Doe, Ray, Me

Memories Eternal

Elizabeth Thompson

Copyright © 2017 Elizabeth Thompson

The moral right of the author has been asserted.

Apart from any fair dealing for the purposes of research or private study, or criticism or review, as permitted under the Copyright, Designs and Patents Act 1988, this publication may only be reproduced, stored or transmitted, in any form or by any means, with the prior permission in writing of the publishers, or in the case of reprographic reproduction in accordance with the terms of licences issued by the Copyright Licensing Agency. Enquiries concerning reproduction outside those terms should be sent to the publishers.

Matador
9 Priory Business Park,
Wistow Road, Kibworth Beauchamp,
Leicestershire. LE8 0RX
Tel: 0116 279 2299
Email: books@troubador.co.uk
Web: www.troubador.co.uk/matador
Twitter: @matadorbooks

ISBN 978 1788036 252

British Library Cataloguing in Publication Data.
A catalogue record for this book is available from the British Library.

Printed and bound in the UK by TJ International, Padstow, Cornwall
Typeset in 11pt Baskerville by Troubador Publishing Ltd, Leicester, UK

Matador is an imprint of Troubador Publishing Ltd

Dedicated to

'Joe'

My Forever Friend.

Acknowledgements

Although there are many people that I would like to thank for giving *Me* the courage and confidence to write this book, the first must be T, my husband, companion and confidant for over thirty-five years. A true friend and partner who has inspired, encouraged and guided *Me* in writing this book and who has helped *Me* to better understand the pathway of my life, listening patiently to many hours of expressive thoughts relating to my earlier childhood and our later life together. For his wisdom and insightfulness, I will be forever indebted. T and I have always lived our personal lives in privacy and we seek your understanding for maintaining our continuing anonymity throughout this book.

Initially, writing this book offered a way to seek and express a greater reflective understanding for *Me*, and a means to capture and articulate my life to my family and friends; to simply record a little of our shared background and history for future generations of family. If my personal journey is discovered by a wider readership through publication, I trust that you too might be inspired to explore your own peace and solace through similarly shared experiences and a personal reflective thoughtfulness within the context of your own life journey.

I have chosen to expand this anonymity by altering names for other extended family members, friends and acquaintances referenced throughout my story, excepting my immediate family for whom this book is primarily written. I trust in their understanding and acceptance that this too enables *Me* to tell our story as a living memory of our shared past time history.

My grateful thanks are extended to each and all named characters for the part that you have played in my life, for the significant influences that you have provided to warrant inclusion; had our paths not crossed, my story may have been measurably diminished.

To my precious son and my treasured daughter, I am eternally grateful for their patience and forbearance in living with and accepting my many eccentricities and in forgiving *Me* for publicly revealing some personal aspects of our shared lives together. I offer this book to you and your future respective families as an inheritance of my love for you both. I can offer no greater gift than the gift of my inner self; the self that is truly *Me*, your mum.

Last but most profoundly, I thank my sister Doe and my brother Ray upon whom this book is entitled and based. Our stories are inextricably entwined. Some of the revealed family truths previously buried or hidden may be painful to read, but the greater healing is through acknowledging truths with compassion and a sought-after understanding for any wrongs inflicted or endured. Only through confronting past hurts in the light of open honesty can we gain a sincere reconciliation for an eternal future with past wrongdoers, whether they be from within our own family or from without.

Our respective recollections may at times differ, but any variances are simply personal perspectives refracted from different angles, whilst looking back through the same glass of time.

Elizabeth

Foreword

When I was a child, I spoke as a child, I understood as a child, I thought as a child; but when I became a (wo)man, I put away childish things. For now, we see in a mirror, dimly, but then face to face. Now I know in part, but then I shall know just as I also am known.

1 Corinthians 13:11-12

I first met *Me* when I was aged just six. A long-time friend of my next-door neighbour was visiting her school friend whom she had not seen for some years and introduced me to her daughter, a beautiful lively girl matching my age with a quirky bob haircut that seemed to frame a radiance and beauty that instantly captured my young heart. We spent but a short afternoon playing, laughing and talking together. I was instantly in love for the first time in my life.

Ten years later, I fell in love for the second time in my life with a beautiful stranger on a bus journey home from school. Only years later still, did we make the earlier connection through shared acquaintances, to realise that my first love was in fact my second love, separated only in time and by memory. Synchronicity or just a double collision of fate. Are we destined to meet our 'soul mates' through this life or simply fortunate to rediscover a lost ticket in the lottery of love?

I have shared the longer part of my life with *Me*. Shared in her love reflected in our children together. In her happiness and laughter, her humour and anger, her physical pain and her emotional distress and sadness. In her resilience and steely determination to overcome adversity in life with a compassion and an immense empathy that surpasses the most basic instinct not to forgive. As her husband, I can be dismissed as biased, but as her closest companion and fellow traveller through a significant part of her life's journey, I am unquestionably best positioned and qualified to attest to the remarkable person who chooses to be simply known within these pages as *Me*.

Me gives us a remarkable story of personal experience, self-discovery and reflective understanding. Through a narrative that flows from the pain of approaching death and separation from a loved one, she takes us on a reflective journey for a life lived. *Me* grants privileged access for each of us to feel and share in very personal emotions of fun and laughter, of pain and despair. *Me* instils freedom to question conventional and conservative thinking that may challenge our own thoughts, feelings and beliefs as we, too, are each immersed in her journey of self-discovery and a greater understanding as to the eternal question, why?

Whether you choose to accept or reject the variable conclusions drawn by *Me* from her life, reflected beneath the emotions and distress of pending death and separation, is not what is most relevant. What is more pertinent is to embrace the power of personal reflection that can help each living soul to draw their own individual peace and understanding before departing this world. To be comforted by the assured knowledge and acceptance that their life, every life, has a purpose and value. That in living our lives we have fulfilled a greater destiny of learning that will elevate us in the continuing spiritual life and existence that exists beyond this realm.

Me does not attempt nor ever wants to present or promote herself as an enlightened or spiritual guide or guru. Quite the opposite. *Me* is simply an ordinary person with ordinary thoughts and emotions but with an extraordinary mindfulness and capacity to explore a greater depth of meaning. *Me* has probed the darker recesses of her experiences to expose uncertainties and insecurities. *Me* has questioned her nurtured beliefs, reopened emotional hurts and physical wounds and laid vulnerable her life, mindful that her treasured privacy may be scrutinised and ridiculed by friends and strangers alike. The courage to undertake such a journey is testament enough to the character that is *Me*. The prize is a privileged insightfulness commonly denied to each one of us until our moment before death and then discovered too late to tell and share.

I stand as a witness for many experiences shared with *Me*. I can vouch for the authenticity of her reflections through conversations held over the course of many years. I find myself challenged too, not by the meaning of life, but by the meaning of my life.

Having read *Doe, Ray, Me*, I feel inspired to examine my own life and experiences through greater personal reflection. To seek the meaning and purpose for my life. To capture for myself the extraordinary assurance that the life I am living is the life that I have chosen to live and that I am living this life to the very best of my ability.

I trust that, in reading *Doe, Ray, Me*, you too might seek to undertake a similar adventure.

T.

Contents

Chapter 1	Doe, Ray, *Me*	1
Chapter 2	The monster in *Me*	10
Chapter 3	Death becomes *Me*	20
Chapter 4	Shame upon *Me*	28
Chapter 5	The fire that scorched *Me*	42
Chapter 6	Out of the fire and into the frying pan for *Me*	50
Chapter 7	To have and to behold *Me*	62
Chapter 8	A new family for *Me*	72
Chapter 9	Angels and feathers surround *Me*	81
Chapter 10	The light comes to *Me*	87
Chapter 11	The carer in *Me*	94
Chapter 12	Teaching *Me*	100
Chapter 13	Reunited – Doe, Ray and *Me*	110
Chapter 14	The loss in *Me*	120
Chapter 15	The jigsaw puzzle that is *Me*	129
Epilogue		132

Chapter 1

Doe, Ray, *Me*

Our brothers and sisters are there with us from the dawn of our personal stories to the inevitable dusk.

Susan Scarf Merrell

Despite sensing that death is preparing to cast its final shroud of darkness, through a numbed detachment, I find myself unexpectedly, yet serenely calm. Minute by minute as the past hours receded, the rhythm of breathing grew shallower until now barely audible. Exhaling like a dry sponge, I somehow expel another pocket of spent air from my lungs, allowing *Me* to soak up a few more precious moments of life. So, this is the end.

    Impending death. Less dramatic than I anticipated, but then Hollywood always created exaggerated theatrics for a more memorable exit. I feel an overwhelming compulsion to hold my breath, to help hasten the inevitable. My heart is pounding. An involuntary salty tear finds a channel to the corner of my mouth giving temporary relief to my parched lips. Through misty eyes, I can make out the outline of my sister, her hand holding a hand in comfort. My brother quite motionless, but somehow at peace with the unfolding trauma engulfing us. Just beyond my peripheral vision, I discern my husband T, quietly muffling his emotions. Real men do cry it seems.

I had often read that your life flashes before you in the moments before death; like a final audit giving account for the life lived and the lessons learned. Just as suddenly as the thought enters my head, I am immersed beneath a tsunami of memories and emotions. Never-ending waves of past experiences wash over *Me*. Each memory rolling over *Me* succeeded by the next, and another, for a life replayed, for a life relived.

A long forgotten yet familiar song from childhood begins to resonate in my mind. I recognise the lyrics immortalised by the voice of Julie Andrews, waxing softly from *The Sound of Music*: 'Do-Re-Mi, Do-Re-Mi'…

> *Doe, a deer, a female deer*
> *Ray, a drop of golden sun*
> *Me, a name I call myself*

Me, I am five years old. I am playing in the back garden of our imposing five-storey town house. Once the old town infirmary, it now serves the Thompson clan as our family home. With *Me* are my sister Doreen, or Doe as I call her and Raymond, or Ray my brother.

> *Doe, Ray, Me.*

Doe is the middle sibling, Ray the eldest and then there is *Me*; the youngest and considered the *wee imp* of the family.

Aptly named, Doe displays the maternal characteristics of a female deer. Instinctively practical, independent of mind and light-footed. Constantly scanning the horizon, watching and protecting, always busy planning what to do and where to roam next.

Ray, a natural font of pure sunlight. Looming large but

mostly anonymously in the background, but forever casting his warmth and light into each of our lives.

And *Me*, the little sister. Curious and mischievous, always chasing fun, laughter and adventure. I find my adventures in abundance, although perhaps not always in the manner that I might have imagined or wanted.

My earliest childhood memory is entwined with growing up within our town house on Saul Street in Downpatrick, one of Ireland's most ancient and historic towns, commonly stated to be the burial place of St. Patrick, the patron saint of Ireland. The town takes its name from the Irish *dún*, which translates as fort and *Pádraig* meaning 'Patrick's stronghold', to form the name *Dún Pádraig* or, as known today, Downpatrick. Spiralling outwards along four thoroughfares, English Street, Irish Street, Scotch Street and Saul Street, each symbolise compass points to the four nations. What appears to be an obvious snub to the Welsh is more cryptically appreciated through the subtlety that St. Patrick was rumoured to have brought Christianity into Ireland from Wales. I like to imagine my street was a special tribute to the apostle Paul, also known as Saul. Special, because it records that St. Patrick, the Welsh Saul, first walked up what is now my street to build his fort on the hill, his pulpit for proclaiming Christianity from an elevated site now established as Down Cathedral.

Our home on Saul Street was converted by local gentry who raised the modest sum of £810 to establish the first County Infirmary in October 1767. The house only served as an infirmary for seven years before moving to larger premises on the then Barrack Lane, now Fountain Street, as patient demands for its services quickly outgrew the town house.

Positioned on the corner of Saul Street, our home captured every child's fantasy, a life-sized playhouse. An imposing five-storey block stone building skewered by a helter-skelter of stairs and banisters linking the attic to the original basement with its now redundant wine cellar. Peering through the half-moon metal barred windows ventilating the cellar enables *Me* to spy unseen onto the street life above.

As young children, we are encouraged not to stray from the house or garden creating a co-dependency that forces *Me* to form my own mystical and magical playground with Doe and Ray. Home on Saul Street provides constant fuel to fire my vivid imagination for escapism and playful adventure.

Plummeting involuntarily into a hypnotic regression, my memory instantly reverts *Me* back to a happier, carefree time and place. A time in childhood where my greatest enemy is an expanse of vacuous time and boredom, an adversary that rarely triumphs due to my active sense of curiosity and mischief. Today I'm challenging myself with a mission to climb to the top of the world's tallest mountain. Four flights of stairs and some countless steps later, I pause breathlessly on the hall landing where I share one of the three adjacent bedrooms with my sister Doe. Sizing up the remaining staircase, the final ascent to the two rooms above, I take a deep breath and bound triumphantly to the summit, but immediately and instinctively hesitate. Caution gravitates *Me* to go towards the room on the right where I can embrace the comfort of familiarity, where my trusty old tricycle waits expectantly to be raced at speed around the empty room unhindered. But curiosity, perhaps emboldened by having just conquered Everest at aged five, teases *Me* to be more daring and courageous and to move left. Drawn to the left, I gingerly push the door open to peer still undecidedly into the dimly lit and, as yet, unexplored abyss beyond. An uncharted chasm that spans the room on the top of the world.

Seemingly empty, but exuding a musty smell of ageless dust and pungent damp, I shuffle hesitantly into the open, chilly void beyond. Gradually, my eyes adjust to the partial light, straining to penetrate from the far gable-wall window;

each pane so dirty that the strong morning sun rays barely stretch back to the doorway. Adjusting to the shadowy light, I can see it, just where Doe said it was. Off-centre and positioned to give approaching advantage over any unwelcome intruders that might dare to steal into his private domain, is Hughie's chair.

Hughie is our resident ghost who lives in the top room, a ghostly relic from the days of the old infirmary. Abandoned when the infirmary was closing, my imagination embellishes the sketchy and lesser known facts about Hughie. The *scary old man who will creep down to the floor below if we make noise before sleep-time*, according to Mummy. The *angry old man who eats little girls who stray into his room* is Doe's take on Hughie.

Designed to instil fear and compliant obedience before bedtime, the sinister threat of Hughie provokes an opposite effect. To *Me*, Hughie is simply an ageing but reclusive patient. Someone overlooked and mistakenly left behind when the infirmary relocated. A harmless old man clinging to the comforting reassurance of his adopted home by hiding in the top room after everyone had left. Slowly Hughie embraced his prevailing insanity by stalking in lonely isolation the upper floorboards of the old infirmary in Saul Street; through the early decades into the endless centuries to follow, until succumbing to an unhealthy possession against ever leaving his self-imposed sanctuary. Today, I am determined to uncover the truth.

Moving hesitantly towards Hughie's chair, my eyes adjusting to the unfamiliar room, I'm abruptly struck by the realisation that the old armchair is unoccupied. Suddenly I sense Hughie standing behind *Me*, his breath low and foul from not having cleaned his teeth for almost two hundred years. My bravado has gone and I'm gripped by a tremendous panic. Doe was right, I'm going to be eaten alive by Hughie. If I don't look at him he won't eat *Me*, I reason.

Quickly retracing my steps, my skin becomes acutely aware of a cold dampness creeping into my pants. Freshly changed earlier this morning, I realise I have wet myself. Temporarily forgetting Hughie, the intruding thought that Daddy is going to kill *Me* ushers in a new distraction. Reaching the door, I spin and bolt down to the floor below, crashing into my room and reaching my bed in a single stride. I burrow myself under the blankets beyond the pursuing grasp of Hughie or Daddy.

Fixating on my spoiled pants, the cinematic reel in my head instantly projects *Me* forward to a balmy afternoon scene in our back garden. Showing off to Ray, who can't climb because of his strange legs, I run down the grassy incline to the tall elm tree that provides a clear view over the perimeter wall and into the rear of the local fire station. Previously, I got to peek at the firemen rescuing a man from the top of a burning inferno, their practice tower, blushing when my cover was exposed by a much younger fireman who waved and smiled at *Me*. Hopefully today I can catch another glimpse of my hero.

Clambering up the tree, I excitedly call back to Ray, *look at Me, look at Me I'm a monkey I can* ... the branch snaps and I tumble through the foliage snagging on a previously amputated lower limb. Hanging precariously by the stretching elasticated waistband around my green cotton school pants, I call to Ray for help, but he giggles and laughs so much that I find myself laughing too, despite my undignified predicament.

Ray, a drop of golden sun, my brother. Born with spina bifida and cerebral palsy, cruelly compounded by contracting meningitis as an infant, Ray can only anticipate a lifetime of trials and tribulations. To *Me*, Ray is the same but different. As a child, I am oblivious to any significant differences, I simply recognise that Ray has a funny walk. He is my big brother, my playmate, my constant companion. As a child, at home, I never hear the words 'disabled' or 'disability'. I instinctively understand, brought up to naturally accept that everyone had differing abilities, physical and mental. Older or younger, smarter or still learning, faster or slower, taller or shorter, blue eyes or brown eyes, blonde hair or red, we are all different but the same. Ray is different from *Me*. I am different from Doe. We three are different from each of our respective friends. At times our differences need a helping hand, a little more time, a greater measure of patience, understanding or tolerance.

Doe, Ray and *Me* bump along together, sometimes bumping into each other and sometimes bumping into others but never with intentional malice or hurtful spite. Many times, I take advantage of Ray's instinctive nature to accept and absorb all blame without protest. Protected by his special place in the pecking order, this allows *Me* to pinch biscuits and to steal coins from Daddy's pockets, knowing that if I was to be found guilty, I would be smacked and sent straight to bed. Ray always plays along with our innocent conspiracy, assured that Daddy will pull a pretend angry face but grant an immediate amnesty. A part of *Me* concedes that Daddy secretly knows. Whether he chooses to find it endearing, or he admires my audacity to make money, albeit by stealing from his pockets, I'll never know.

Not all children are like Doe, Ray and *Me*; some are positively cruel and spiteful.

My eyes well with tears as my mind recalls a particularly harrowing time for poor Ray at school. Beyond the protection of family, Ray tries so hard to blend in with everyone else at school; striving to the best of his limited abilities to be simply accepted and included by everybody. Daddy, in an unpredictable way, is ahead of his time by resisting the pressures to place Ray in a special school, insisting that Ray is enrolled in mainstream education to be integrated with all the other kids his age. *Special schools are the gateway to institutions and my son is never to be institutionalised. Institutions are for mad or bad people. My son is not mad or bad,* he rages. Ray is encouraged and pushed to make the best of his abilities. An aspiration readily embraced today, but neither the school nor the pupils are equipped or sufficiently progressive to deal with his special learning needs in the 1960s and Ray pays a heavy price for trying to compete equally within an inequitable education system. Ray becomes as much a sporting outcast, barred from taking part in school football, as a social misfit, who it is commonly thought might hinder fun if invited to attend school friends' birthday parties.

Ray immediately attracts attention from the playground bullies simply for being perceived as different. He is picked upon by a gang of boys and made the butt of endless jokes, laughed and spat at, punched, poked, prodded and kicked. His worst abusers taunt and threaten Ray, forcing him to regularly expose his 'willy' in front of the other boys and girls, risking a severe beating should he refuse to strip. Desperate, frightened and in a futile attempt to be accepted, Ray endures the regular humiliation, failing to understand that being the centre of attention is not the same as peer acceptance. His manipulation regrettably escalates to taunting accusations across the wider school for being a 'perv'; a disparaging and shaming name-tag wholly undeserved, and one that persistently inhibits Ray's progress throughout his unhappy time in secondary school.

Fortunately, just as every bad thing is balanced by something equally good, yin and yang, a Good Samaritan crosses Ray's path. David, a slightly older boy with a strong Christian faith and guiding principles, recognises both the cruelty and the injustice being cynically targeted and perpetrated against Ray. Risking his own safety and reputation, he chooses to cross the road to care for and to help protect Ray against his own vulnerabilities. David's intervention is beyond the maturity of his peers as he commits to make practical efforts and personal sacrifices to look out for Ray, a gesture that gradually gains Ray temporary respite from his abusers. Perhaps born initially out of pity or sympathy, his guardianship evolves into a befriending relationship built upon genuine empathy and mutual respect that helps Ray to recover a little of his self-respect and self-esteem. David maintains a distance contact and relationship with Ray long after their schooling takes them off in different directions. Ray's school life continues to be challenging, constantly alternating from apathy through to hostility, but at least for a short but critical few years, Ray has his own biblical David to help him slay the threatening 'Philistines'.

At home, Doe and Ray's personalities and temperaments bump most often, although at times their interactions could more accurately be described as collisions. Whether because of Doe's stubborn instincts to dominate and control, or Ray's tendency and ability to wind Doe up like a timepiece until she springs on cue, I can never be sure, but on frequent occasions hair literally does fly. I suspect that each is as provoking as the other but it certainly adds an unpredictable rising ingredient into our siblings' mix. Doe is the mother hen, taking on a premature role for cooking and cleaning, organising and disciplining, and I can be forgiven for sometimes being confused as to who is the mummy within the house. Behind Doe's back, I affectionately name her 'old bossy boots', a pet name that sticks with Ray and *Me* and one that seems to prophesy her maturing character and personality.

Seamlessly, and without any ability to control my thoughts, my mind glides effortlessly forward into my seventh year.

What we remember from childhood we remember forever –
permanent ghosts, stamped, inked, imprinted, eternally seen.
Cynthia Ozick

Chapter 2

The monster in *Me*

Your memory is a monster; you forget – it doesn't. It simply files things away. It keeps things for you, or hides things from you – and summons them to your recall with a will of its own. You think you have a memory; but it has you!

John Irving, A Prayer for Owen Meany, 1989

To *Me*, Daddy stirs a cocktail of feelings and emotions. As my father, I feel and experience his paternal love and I reciprocate with a daughter's love and yet my earliest memories are clouded with conflicting passions of hate, anger, confusion and fear. Daddy embodies a paradox of personalities and dark mysteries that play havoc with my young developing mind, given its limited capacity to fully understand. Thinking about the contradictions sends my head into a kaleidoscope of memories; each separated in time, but fusing together to give *Me* a more complete picture and a better appreciation for the legacy of emotional scars that have shaped and coloured my relationship with Daddy and my feelings towards him. Feelings that have long survived his death.

This kaleidoscope immediately intrudes into my mind a vision, ostensibly ordinary and mundane. The picture that comes into focus shows our family whiling away a Saturday afternoon at home in the living room. Ray is curled up on an armchair quietly reading to himself from one of his favourite poetry books. Doe is slumbering on the sofa recovering from the morning housekeeping chores and Mummy is elsewhere; in the kitchen, I think, preparing for evening dinner. Daddy seems engrossed watching afternoon football broadcasts on our new colour television. *Me*, I'm sitting cross-legged opposite the open coal fire, humming and softly singing along to the latest popular release.

Vaguely aware that Daddy seems to be becoming increasingly agitated by my singing, I tone it down until it becomes barely audible, even to *Me*. Suddenly, without warning, the tranquillity of my world explodes as Daddy lunges forward from his armchair, grasps the blackened poker from the fireplace hearth and flings it like a sound-seeking missile in my direction. Narrowly missing my head, but leaving an ugly indent on the wall behind, I couldn't fail to feel the sting from the venomous *I told you to be quiet* aftershock that reverberates in my ears. Stunned into silence for having the audacity to disrupt his football viewing, I sit motionless, gripped by a paralysing fear that becomes my stock reaction in life when confronted by any threatening situation or experience.

Doe breaks my silent paralysis by dashing from the room, bolting up the stairs towards our bedroom retreat, hotly pursued by *Me* as I strive to overtake her lead on the third floor. No thought for poor Ray who has probably tried to cloak himself invisible behind an inward recital of verse by his favourite Thomas Hardy, or perhaps more ironically, Wilfred Owen's *Anthem for Doomed Youth*.

Crossing the finishing line fractionally behind Doe, we each bury ourselves beneath the blankets, a shield from further assault. Doe creeps to the bottom, wedging between the footplate and my body, threatening to hold her breath until she suffocates, and I thought I was the drama queen. It did, however, have a distracting effect; the thought of losing Doe a greater trauma for *Me* than continuing to fret and worry about Daddy or what he might or might not do next. What I didn't expect was what Mummy did next.

Having managed to avoid and not speak a word to Daddy by hiding away in my bedroom, the following morning I hear Mummy and Daddy whispering from down the corridor in their bedroom. Worried that another argument is brewing that might end with Mummy getting hurt, I quietly sneak past Ray's room to discreetly listen at their bedroom door. I can't hear what's being said so I drop down onto my knees, allowing *Me* to put my eye to the small space between the door frame and the slightly opened door. Mummy is lying on the bed with Daddy beside her, both fully clothed, and they are kissing and cuddling. Daddy is stroking Mummy's hair and whispering in her ear as he continues to kiss the side of her neck. Mummy is smiling and making a funny noise like a cat purring. I feel strange butterflies dancing around in my stomach before indignation distracts *Me*. How could she? She knows what Daddy did to *Me* and she's being really nice to him. I scamper back to my own bed and bury my face deep into the pillows and cry. Feeling totally alone and abandoned, I cry and cry until exhaustion and sleep dry my tears.

My daddy, Charlie Thompson, was a generation older than Mummy by some twenty-two years. Although not a particularly tall or distinguished man, he did command a presence and an authority that sat comfortably with his Victorian attitude to family life and discipline. Beyond discovering in later years that he was one of seven siblings, his family history and earlier life remained a shrouded mystery or perhaps a conspiracy of secrecy. Following his death, a couple of years after the poker incident, I am again stunned into shock and silence to discover, through eavesdropping into a conversation at his wake, that Daddy had another wife, Dorothy. The undertaker, old Morris, is gushing excitedly about the privilege of burying Charlie, having also buried his first wife Dorothy. Daddy was married before Mummy. My goodness, did Mummy know? Did Daddy and Dorothy have children? Have I got a stepsister, suddenly remembering a black and white photograph that I once discovered showing a much younger, dark-haired Charlie, sporting a tidy moustache and standing beside a very pretty lady? A young girl, perhaps about ten years of age, is holding hands, standing between Daddy and Dorothy. Even long after his death, fading recollections of Daddy can send my mind into an automatic whirlwind. The undertaker, now on a roll with a captive audience, then adds spice to his privileged insight. Disclosing the lamentable fact that *Dorothy of course died an alcoholic*, he alludes to the distress and embarrassment that this must have caused to poor Charlie. The whirlwind would have spiralled into a tornado had I known then how Mummy would succumb to alcoholism too. Was Daddy some kind of monster that drove both his wives to alcohol addiction and premature deaths?

Charlie Thompson had established his position as a successful and enterprising businessman before he met and later married Annie Blevins, Mummy. How he made and amassed his rumoured fortune was, as most things in Charlie's life, a mystery, although gossiped to have been leveraged from Dorothy's inheritance as an only child. From a working-class background, Charlie was financially secure by the time he met Annie. Beyond his ownership of the Black and White garage in Downpatrick, from where he also operated a small but successful taxi business, Charlie was a secretive but prolific speculator in stocks, shares and bonds. By middle age he had acquired money, reputation and prestige through his business acumen, but lacked the social acceptance and passage that only a wife could provide and a family to whom he could bequeath his growing estate.

Annie Blevins fitted the profile. Young, fertile and attractive, from a modest if not slightly impoverished background, and yet hungry and ambitious for the financial security and social advantages that a much younger man might fail to provide. Not known in local circles around Downpatrick, 'emigrating' from the rural community of Annaghmore eight miles west of Portadown in County Armagh, Annie suited Charlie's penchant for keeping the background to his affairs, business and personal, private. It was a marriage, if not of unbridled love, certainly one of mutual convenience.

Mummy delivered on her part of the marriage contract by giving to Charlie his desired family, Doe, Ray and *Me*.

Charlie and Annie had a tempestuous life together. Annie may have brought what Charlie sought to the marriage, but she also introduced youthfulness and a strong sense of independence of mind that tested and challenged Charlie's aspirations for a quiet and dutiful wife. A 'Stepford' wife Annie was not, nor ever would be.

Although roughly equal in height, Annie appeared tall, slim and elegant, emphasising Charlie to appear shorter and stouter. Standing together they passed more as father and daughter than husband and wife. Annie was kind, sensitive and generous, a budgetary challenge as her purse strings were always strictly controlled by Charlie's inherent meanness with the housekeeping allowance. As children, we could be found withering from thirst on the front steps, watching with envy as the other children enjoyed their flavoured ice lollies and whipped ice creams on a hot Sunday afternoon. *If you're thirsty there's plenty of water in the tap*, was Daddy's stock response. Mummy would disappear upstairs, returning to wait her moment until Daddy was distracted, usually on the toilet having his 'after-lunch constitution', whatever that was. This closeting behind closed doors enabled Mummy to then slip some coins to each of us to buy a fruit-flavoured ice lolly; money, I assumed, that came from her secret 'rainy day fund'. Too mean to pay for us to go to the hairdressers for a professional haircut, Daddy took charge to personally style each of our hairs exactly the same. A ceramic soup bowl tilted slightly backwards on the top of our heads with the length and fringe cut to meet the edge of the bowl; Daddy's technique for styling a fashionable neat 'bob'. It certainly saved him a bob or two.

Mummy, to my recollection, seemed to be happy nevertheless, always busying herself in the kitchen, the garden or with friends. Mummy was just like everyone else's mummy, at least during my earliest years. As parents, they occasionally took us out together as a family. Once, whilst Mummy prepared the picnic, Daddy taught *Me* how to ride a proper grown-up's bicycle, *not that silly tricycle that you waste so much of your time on*, he teased. It must have seemed comical to anyone passing to see *Me* struggling to balance without stabilisers and having to learn to cycle by standing on the pedals. I was far too short to properly sit and pedal, so Daddy held onto the seat from behind, pushing, shoving, shouting and panting as he struggled to teach *Me* the finer points of cycling. Probably saved money to go straight from a tricycle to a bike sized for a teenager, I cynically concluded. Overdressed in his usual heavy dark woollen business suit, Daddy more resembled the butler from a classic period drama, despatched to the park by his master to instruct the young lady of the house on how to cycle; a far cry from the young dads today, bedecked in their branded sportswear, coaching and encouraging their sons and daughters to cycle.

On other occasions, we all headed off in Daddy's prized black Ford Zephyr that he named Bert, bought with the brown paper bag. Every time Daddy purchased anything of value, his cars, coal from across the border in what was referred to then as the Irish Free State, the new colour television, one of the very first in Downpatrick, Daddy always set off with a wad of bank notes in a brown paper bag. *I don't trust banks*, he often muttered, a weakness in how he managed his financial affairs that was to puzzle *Me* long after his death when his 'fortune' could not be fully accounted for.

Most family car journeys were to visit aunts and uncles in either Coleraine, close to the North Antrim coast, or in the opposite direction into Belfast, where we would spend the day with our cousins. Three boys as different in character as could be possible for siblings, but also from Doe, Ray and *Me*. Ray and I loved Coleraine, particularly when visiting Uncle Lou and Auntie Kitty, Daddy's brother and sister-in-law. Although instructed to be seen and not heard, we were always captivated by Auntie Kitty who was bags of fun and told such animated stories that kept us giggling for hours long after we returned home and had gone to bed.

Belfast was different. Uncle Billy was my favourite uncle, a butcher by trade who loved to spend his time entertaining us along with his three boys, leaving the grown-up talk to his wife Dorothy who could talk for Ireland. Although not properly our aunt and uncle, Dorothy being Daddy's niece, as children we always knew Dorothy and Billy as our aunt and uncle, making their boys our only cousins. Doe seemed to like Auntie Dorothy the most, despite her obsessive tendency to constantly clean and dust around everyone whilst telling them about her latest medical problems. Doe showed an unnatural interest and enthusiasm for Auntie Dorothy's many and varied ailments, following every word to a level that must have qualified her medically to know the route from Dorothy's stomach through her bowels and around her kidneys better than any doctor. Dorothy had a sister Edith who lived in Somerset with her English husband Robert who both occasionally visited and who developed a particular interest in Doe that was to cause a major family upset in later years.

Mummy always came alive when Daddy organised to visit her old stomping ground in Annaghmore, a world away from the middle-class homes in Coleraine and Belfast. Visiting Freddie and Ethel, Mummy's uncle and aunt, always stirred feelings of coming home, of belonging. Despite their modest home, a small traditional whitewashed tailor's cottage with an outside toilet, make-do furniture and lifestyle, Auntie Ethel's home was reputed to be the cleanest and most welcoming in the district, if not the county. Doe, Ray and *Me* always got the biggest welcome followed by hugs and cuddles and laughter all round. Great Uncle Edward, Grandad's brother, a neighbour to Uncle Freddie and Auntie Ethel, kept a donkey called Zippy that he hitched up to an old delivery cart with its flaking red and green painted livery along the sides. Uncle Freddie took Doe, Ray and *Me* for what he called a *canter* around the country lanes. I don't think Uncle Freddie or Zippy ever knew what speed a canter was as even Ray could outpace the old beast.

After an hour circling the cottage, we returned to the smell of freshly-baked fruit scones, Auntie Ethel's signature recipe. The scones were simply to die for when served hot and smothered in salted butter from the old sage-green-coloured Aga that dominated the corner of the living room. Even now, thinking about Auntie Ethel, I go all nostalgic and can smell freshly-baked scones. I devoured, too, the family stories that Auntie Ethel brought into our lives, especially those that involved Grandad who apparently ran a bicycle repair business and the early years' stories of my Uncle Jimmy, Mummy's only brother, who now drove big delivery lorries around the country. My favourite stories were about Mummy as a naughty child and teenager who ran off at fifteen years of age to lie about her age so as to be accepted into the Women's

Royal Air Force; seeking thrills and adventures that would *never come her way had she stayed in Annaghmore and married a local man,* according to Auntie Ethel.

Much as I loved to visit our relatives, I always dreaded the car journeys back to home. Inevitably the excitement of the outward journey and the fun and laughter I enjoyed with my aunts, uncles and cousins, differed from Mummy and Daddy's experience as they always seemed to argue on the homeward journeys. The common thread appeared to be something one of my aunts or uncles said or did that caused offence and provoked a disagreement. One such argument lasted the whole of the journey home continuing into the house, although it seemed to *Me* to simply go around and around in circles with neither Daddy nor Mummy willing to concede defeat or at least compromise. What happened next brought the disagreement to a decisive end but ignited an estrangement between *Me* and Daddy that was left unresolved.

I have no idea what exactly was said or done or by whom, as I had long since retreated into my private world of happy places, but I do know who was guilty of pulling the trigger. Daddy, because I had seen him do it. With lightning speed, Daddy's right hand shoots across the space separating him from Mummy followed by what sounds to *Me* like a loud clap of thunder making Mummy's face spin violently, sending her reading glasses flying past *Me*, shattering on impact with the wall; so forceful is Daddy's slap delivered.

Nothing further is said. Nothing was ever said about it again. Mummy quietly cries. I can't cry, my paralysis takes over again, but inside I am screaming through burning tears *you monster, you monster. Monster, monster, monster...* Daddy takes back control by quietly but assertively telling us *to go to bed.* Lacking the courage to confront him, I get up, abandon my mummy in her moment of need and go quietly to bed. Tomorrow will be my seventh birthday.

My whole body goes into spasm, I can feel droplets of sweat trickling down my face and a rising sense of panic as my head explodes with memories no longer in chronological order, seemingly random but somehow connected. I'm drowning in waves of emotions that are physically choking *Me*. Just when I think I'm about to pass out, an inner voice breaks through my impending unconsciousness. *Stop fighting. Embrace your memories. Understand their meaning and learn from the life you have lived, the life that you chose.*

Just as suddenly as it begins I'm floating on a different sea of calmness. A new clarity comes into my consciousness. *The life I chose.* I chose this life to live. I wrote the narrative, someone or something else doesn't write this narrative for my life. The choices I make, the decisions I take, each designed to teach *Me* what I need to learn. The final lessons to be learnt, to be taught through self-reflection. Only by joining up the memory dots can I begin to more fully see and understand the completed picture of what was and is my life.

In the moment of living each of my experiences, I stand abstractly behind the personal tapestry that is my life unfolding. From behind, observing my life, it appears as a mess of seemingly unconnected threads and knots. I realise now that I can only properly review my fuller life by stepping around, by standing and reviewing my life from the front, to see and appreciate the emerging picture that is *Me*.

Initially I can only see and understand in part, but gradually over time I can see more of my life picture emerging in a gloriously and vibrant technicolour.

I become who I am only when I fully understand *Me*.

Oh yes, the past can hurt. But, you can either run from it or learn from it.
 – from the movie The Lion King

Chapter 3

Death becomes *Me*

It is important to feel the anger without judging it, without attempting to find meaning in it. It may take many forms: anger at life, at your loved one for leaving. Life is unfair. Death is unfair. Anger is a natural reaction to the unfairness of loss.

Elisabeth Kübler-Ross

Not every car journey with Daddy ends badly. One Saturday morning Daddy asks *Me* if I would like to accompany him to pick up a fare and on the return journey we can have a drive along the coast road to Ardglass, on the south County Down coast. With little else to do I agree and make ready to jump into the back seat of the Zephyr when Daddy calls to *Me* over the car roof, to *sit in the front seat*. I hesitate, this isn't usual. Daddy always makes *Me* sit in the back behind his driver's seat. The front seats are only for grown-ups. *Front seat now* he commands. Suspiciously I climb up into the front seat barely able to see over the long bonnet and wait expectantly to see what will happen next. *Only this once*, Daddy qualifies, *I need to pick up a woman from town and take her out to Ardglass to visit her sister. She'll sit in your seat today.* She must be a very tiny woman if she needs to sit in my seat for *Me* to be promoted to sit in the front seat. The journey hardly begins before Daddy parks up outside a small two up two down mid-terrace house on a steep hill just past the town police station. Daddy toots the car horn and this tall woman immediately appears from behind a red door. The woman seems to *Me*, to somehow simultaneously close her front door as she manages to open the rear car door before slipping into the rear seat behind Daddy. All achieved without uttering a single word. Daddy glances up to the rectangular mirror stuck against the middle of the car windscreen and nods. Feeling I need to do something too I turn in my seat and nod to the woman. Just enough to snatch a glimpse but I immediately register three things. The woman is wearing a black coat fully buttoned from under her chin down to her knees. She is wearing a black hat with a small black net attached to the rim that makes it difficult to see her eyes. She is wearing a false nose.

I don't mean a long, pointed witch's nose, although she is dressed a bit like a witch; I mean a proper nose, clearly not her real nose but a proper-shaped nose. Still pondering the nose, the car sets off heading away from Downpatrick onto the main road that goes straight through to Ardglass, a small fishing village seven miles away, according to the traffic sign. Picking up speed on the straight road, Daddy accelerates the car up to thirty miles an hour; he must be in a big hurry to deliver the woman in the back seat.

The woman sneezes, at least I think it was a sneeze because it sounds completely different from the way I sneeze. I can't resist a second look and, as I turn again, I just catch another quick glimpse of her nose. The sneeze has pushed it slightly up her face, almost between her eyes, but before she manages to raise the handkerchief held in her right hand up to her face, I see the two small holes. Dark, almost black in colour around the edges, contrasting against the pale complexion of her cheeks, but definitely two holes right in the middle of her face. I make a noise as I gasp involuntarily before swinging back around in my seat pretending to stare absent-mindedly over the bonnet ahead. A black bonnet, a black dress, black holes, a... Daddy breaks my train of thought with the most withering look that I've ever received, and I've had quite a few of those from Daddy. I don't need to be told, no words are necessary, I instinctively understand. I shouldn't have looked at the woman. I shouldn't have seen the black holes.

Don't look again, Daddy's stare tells *Me*. I won't and I don't, but I do wish that I could explain to Daddy, but I can't. I didn't gasp because I'm shocked or horrified at what I saw. I gasped because it was simply so unexpected. I was simply curious; it was my first encounter with disfigurement but it wouldn't be my last. In the silence that marked the remainder of the journey I think about all the different ways that the woman in the back of our car might have lost her nose. It could have been bitten off by robbers, chopped off when she closed her front door too quickly, eaten by spiders while she slept. I never do find out the real reason as Daddy is clearly not going to give her secret away.

After Daddy drops the woman off at her sister's house, we head into Ardglass village and Daddy parks the car at the small harbour to look at the fishing boats tied up along the inside harbour wall. Nothing is said about the woman. Whatever happened didn't happen. That was Daddy's way. I never get to see the woman again, although I later find out that Daddy made the same journey once a month.

My eighth birthday in April is a low-key event; not that I have any expectation that my school friends will be allowed to visit for a party. Even within the family, it is barely acknowledged and certainly given no memorable celebration to mark the occasion. It does, however, start the stopwatch that sets off a noticeable deterioration in Daddy's health. Over the next six months, Daddy begins to spend longer periods in his bed, increasingly only rising to attend critical hospital appointments. Occasionally, an appointment includes a *sleep-over*, as Mummy refers to his absence for one or two nights. Something Daddy has never done. Before his illness, Daddy was always habitually back home each night, the first to rise and the last to bed. The house adopts an eerie quietness and the atmosphere within becomes increasingly subdued, despite an unusual increase in the number of friends and relatives that call almost daily at the house to whisper to Mummy before visiting Daddy in his bedroom. During this time a builder visits regularly to update Daddy on the progress of our new house that is being built on Saul Road in the suburbs of Downpatrick. Any excitement for our new bungalow is overshadowed by what I again eavesdrop to be Charlie's Big C. I don't have any idea what Daddy's Big C is, but I understand enough that Big C is likely to stop Daddy from moving into our new home after it is completed. I rack my brains to think of anybody named C that could be big enough or brave enough to stand up to Daddy so as to stop him moving house with us. As the months slowly progress I come to realise, without being explicitly told, that Big C is a serious illness called cancer, an illness that Daddy might not survive.

During this time, Mummy becomes more and more distant and estranged from Doe, Ray and *Me*, detached from cooking for us, cleaning the house, generally everything. Increasingly away from the house but even when at home, Mummy is always *too stressed* to do this or that now. Doe steps into the vacuum that is left, assuming her new role as our ten-year-old stepmum. I feel that 'old bossy boots' is enjoying her maternal role with its greater authority over Ray and *Me* too much, but at least she is bringing some much-needed stability and normality into our lives during this time. At the end of September, Uncle Lou and Auntie Kitty come to stay with us at Saul Street. Auntie Kitty is a wonderful distraction, managing to completely shield us from the gravity of Daddy's deteriorating health. For the first time in a very long time I feel happier and spoilt. Auntie Kitty buys *Me* a new pair of fluffy pink slippers and I perform for all like a musical star prancing around the house kicking my legs high in the air for anyone and everyone to see and applaud.

On 12th October 1969 the dragon is finally slain. He hadn't run away with a third wife or been taken by Big C. According to the doctor he died from a massive heart attack. Daddy dies at the premature age of sixty-four leaving Mummy widowed at only forty-three years of age to look after his three children, the oldest Ray just twelve years of age.

Daddy's funeral makes little impact on *Me*. Whether too young or too innocently naïve, I get dressed as instructed, sit in the back of a stranger's large car as directed, also black, and quietly watch as the countryside passes *Me* by on the two-hour drive from Downpatrick to the cemetery in Coleraine where Daddy's coffin is interred. He's *gone on a journey and won't be returning* I am told. I know that I should feel something, but I simply feel nothing. No pain, no loss, just a strange emptiness. A hunger pain that cannot be satisfied by eating.

As I reflect now I feel an immense sadness, an overwhelming grief and loss for the mourning that I missed. A mourning that might have brought closure to the burden of anger, frustration and resentment that I have carried beyond my father's grave. Four decades of acquired wisdom that only maturity and a life more fully lived provides, rushes into the still open and festering wound that is my daddy. It pours a healing ointment, more gentle and persuasive than is my natural instinct to understand or my own ability to accept his shortcomings. I realise that I have condemned and defined my father's memory over my lifetime for essentially two acts of uncharacteristic violence. I realise that we are each and all guilty of making more than a few mistakes over the course of our lives, some as damaging to others as to ourselves for the act of making them. I ask *Me, are we to be defined for all time, throughout all eternity, by and for our few mistakes. Am I to condemn Me for my mistakes too?* A reconciling peace pours a new and fresh healing over the wounds that I held Daddy to account for, but, although it brings comfort, it carries a cautionary caveat.

 I can receive a more lasting peace through a better understanding that leads to reconciliation and forgiveness, but only if I have truly learnt not to re-pick at the scars of past hurts and pain. To do otherwise risks that the healing will be undone and that the wound may again become infectious to *Me* and consequently to those around *Me*.

 I don't excuse some of my father's actions but I do discover a new perspective. Daddy was a man shaped by his life choices too. A man moulded by his generation and their sometimes-prevailing Victorian attitudes to discipline, to life values, marriage and children. Yes, my father did love *Me*, just as he loved Doe and Ray and Mummy. I can see this now in the hundreds and thousands of smaller words, actions and gestures that he bestowed upon each of us, his immediate family, his wider family circle and his community. What I see now too, that I could not see then, nor understand at the time, is the wider context of each individual act that is performed. Had I fully known and understood just how ill my father was becoming, how intolerably frustrating and irritating my repetitive singing may have been on that Saturday afternoon and chosen to play and sing in another room in the house, Daddy would not have thrown the poker. An act out of character that I'm now sure was never actually intended to physically hurt but simply to vent, albeit inappropriately, his acute frustration. When Daddy lashed out to slap Mummy, had I known then what I lived to experience personally as to Mummy's extremely persistent and provocative nature, I might have better understood his uncharacteristic reaction.

A reaction and action perhaps born simply out of pure frustration and exasperation. Mummy could test the patience of any and every saint and Daddy never professed to be a saint.

I still don't condone or excuse any form of physical or mental violence and wish now with all my heart that Daddy could have found a different means to express himself, but I can and do find a new mitigation and forgiveness in my heart. If life is too long to carry a grudge, to carry it for all eternity will be absolutely back-breaking. The realisation that had I thought or chosen to react differently myself, the negative feelings unjustly harboured, the immature assumptions and conclusions that have poisoned my buried memories towards my daddy for over four decades, could so easily have been reconciled. Through my life's review I now realise that very few things are absolute, black or white, totally right or wrong, yes or no. Life is more generally lived in the infinitely wider, greyer spaces.

Even as children, our DNA appears to be programmed to instinctively capture and hold the high ground of moral and ethical judgement against others. Following my own analogy, I can see how my seeking the high ground is self-justified as a defensive position but invariably is abused as a position of judgement. It seems to *Me* that the top of a mountain, the highest ground, can become a cold and barren place to dwell. To reside too long may create the illusion of having the overview to look down upon others but frequently this perspective is obscured by the lower clouds moving around. The longer we remain the more detached and isolated we become. Restricted or starved of oxygen we can become more and more disorientated, if not delusional, with little or no proper balance or sense of perspective.

Conversely, to remain deep down in the valley can be an equally cold, dark and lonely place to exist. Either extreme offers little growth, cold comfort and a limiting view of life. We should strive to climb clear of the darker valleys but remain on the fertile slopes and terraces at the foot of the mountain where we can enjoy all the fruits of this world, to be freely nurtured and replenished by nature's flowing mountain streams.

On the high ground, we fall into the trap of judging others, but rarely question or challenge ourselves, our own actions and our own motives. The lower ground allows seasonal uncertainties and self-doubts to take root that encourage us to question ourselves more and the actions and behaviours of others less. In my quest to understand my father, I can now see many characteristics and traits that belonged to him reflected in *Me*.

Do I believe that this makes *Me* a monster too? No, I do not believe that we are genetically predisposed to repeat the mistakes of our parents.

When you judge another, you do not define them, you define yourself.

Wayne Dyer.

Chapter 4

Shame upon *Me*

Hard times build determination and inner strength. Through them we can also come to appreciate the uselessness of anger. Instead of getting angry nurture a deep caring and respect for troublemakers because by creating such trying circumstances they provide us with invaluable opportunities to practice tolerance and patience.

Dalai Lama XIV

Recalling words spoken by the Reverend at Daddy's funeral service, *and in death we shall find life and find it more abundantly*, I see now how I over-enthusiastically embraced the new-found freedoms and opportunities that emerged without Daddy's controlling but stabilising influence. Just as the house curtains were drawn back from the windows at Saul Street, so too were the curtains drawn back to let a new light shine into our lives. Auntie Kitty, leaving to return to her own home two days after Daddy's funeral hugged *Me* tight, kissed *Me* on my cheek before whispering in my ear, *now that your daddy has departed*, how everybody now referred to his death, *it's time to be a big grown-up girl*. And then she was gone. Departed too, but not like Daddy.

Time to *find life and to find it more abundantly.* For my first excursion as a grown-up I approach Mummy and seek to capture her attention by boldly addressing her as 'Mum'. Even to my ears it sounds very strange, but more grown up. *Mum, can we go shopping for a pair of long trousers?* Bracing myself to be rebuked from beyond the grave, Daddy believed firmly that only men should wear trousers and that women wore skirts and dresses. Mum looks at *Me* pensively for a long time and then, with a smile, replies, *yes dear, what a good idea, I think I need a pair too.* The genie was out of the bottle and a new fashion diva is born. What I don't realise is that Mum has already jumped head first into an even more destructive bottle. Mum takes *Me* into town and I become the proud owner of my first pair of brown flared trousers, all the rage amongst the trendsetters in the seventies. Over the next few years my wardrobe begins to bulge with clothes and accessories as I experiment with my new passion. Determined that I am to be a top fashion buyer after I leave school, in the meantime I decide selfishly but unashamedly that Mum can bankroll my apprenticeship. Although I fail to professionally achieve this aspiration, it does provide a vocational lifeline over many difficult and trying years ahead.

The most significant watershed following Daddy's 'departure' involves saying goodbye to Saul Street. The bungalow on Saul Road, that had its foundations laid before Daddy was diagnosed with cancer, is now completed and organised chaos ensues as we prepare for the house move. Moving from a five-storey house to a three-bedroom split-level bungalow necessitates more than a little downsizing. Mum, in her now familiar care-not attitude, sells or gives away virtually all our solid wooden period furniture that so characterised Saul Street. Furniture chosen and paid for by Daddy, that was designed and crafted to survive the generations but now consigned by Mum to be out of vogue for what is to become our new contemporary style of living on Saul Road.

Too young to appreciate or care about the stress of helping with organising and settling into our new home, I put all my energy into exploring the new neighbourhood and getting to know the other kids on the road. Much to my surprise I am immediately accepted into a small, tightly established gang, despite being the new kid on the block. This is mostly because the leader of the pack, Chris, takes a romantic notion to *Me*, spending the next eight years pursuing more than just a friendship, only to have his heart broken time and time again. Life couldn't be any different. Completing primary school and transferring through my eleven-plus examinations into the Grammar or Down High School as it is called, breezes by in my clear blue sky. Going into my teenage years, I am so wrapped up in finding *life more abundantly*, meeting and partying with friends, learning to smoke and drink alcohol, leading the fashion trends around the town that I fail to see the storm clouds gathering on the horizon once more. So wrapped up in my new life, in *Me*, I completely and quite selfishly lose sight of how Doe and Ray's lives are developing or how Mum is coping without Daddy.

Ray finishes his primary schooling and transfers to secondary level education, completing his education at sixteen without any formal qualifications. Mum secures him a resident place at the Thomas Doran Training Centre at Parkanaur in Dungannon, County Tyrone. Located over forty miles from Downpatrick, Ray enrols as a weekly Monday to Friday boarder, returning home for weekends. Probably because he is away from home on a weekly basis, out of sight and out of mind, this reduces my time with Ray more and more to contact akin to a distant cousin relationship. A far cry from the *big brother, best playmate, and constant companion* he was to *Me* through my earlier childhood years in Saul Street.

At weekends Ray becomes more and more of a stranger in his own home. With no friends to speak off in Downpatrick and a life unknown to *Me* in Dungannon, Ray lives an increasingly shadowy existence. Now you see him, now you don't. Here in body but not in mind or spirit. His personality and temperament changes. Not so much immediately but gradually over time. His happy-go-lucky nature, his spontaneous laughs and giggles, his smile, his chirpy chit-chat, melting away and nobody notices. Not Mum, not Doe, not *Me*. We are each caught up in our respective new lives; Daddy's departure removing the glue that once bonded us together as a family.

The first time Ray exploded I am more bemused than shocked. From the mild-mannered, ever the gentleman Ray, spews a litany of foul and abusive language. Such is the anger and rage that he physically shakes and snarls like a person possessed. Through gritted teeth he repeats, as much to himself as anyone that might remotely care to listen, *I'm not going back, I'm not going back, I'm not going back...*

The first few times Mum manages to quieten Ray with a firm, non-negotiable telling-off. *Yes you are, stop that disgusting talk now, you're going back and that's final.* Everything goes back towards normality, temporarily for a month or two but then Ray, the volcano, starts to erupt again, spewing venomous polluting abuse towards anyone within reach or earshot. As Ray's behaviour worsens, so too does Mum's reaction and response. Hearing Ray starting to vent from a different room in the house, I suspend coordinating my outfits for the weekend ahead to go and act as an intermediary to keep the peace. Just as I walk into the sitting room, Mum completely loses it with Ray. Screaming *I can't cope with this any more*, she starts slapping and smacking Ray uncontrollably across his face and around his head. Each blow as violent and painful as the one slap that I witnessed Daddy landing on Mummy. *Stop it, stop it, stop it!* I scream at the top of my voice. The hypnotic blindness caused by my new, exciting and carefree life is broken and shattered as I race across the room to rescue Ray. I physically push Mum aside and screech for her to get out of the room. I wrap my arms around my *big brother, my forgotten best playmate, and lost constant companion,* and together we cry.

It takes *Me* years, decades, before I can gently and sensitively tease some of the reasons for his uncharacteristic outbursts out of Ray; at least as much of the full truth as he is ever prepared to share. Initially, he starts to open up a little to talk about how he misses his daddy, the daddy he totally adored. *We all miss him,* I lied to help reassure him. I realise more and more just how traumatic Daddy's death has been on Ray, such a huge influence that was taken away from his life without warning or explanation. At the time, because Ray presented his usual happy disposition, we all fell short of recognising the underlying hurt and pain. We were all guilty of putting our own thoughts and feelings, our needs and wants, our new hopes and aspirations first. Ray was left to try and heal the massive wound to his heart without as much as a sticking plaster to help him.

Struggling in quiet isolation with his emotional trauma, Ray's physical world is then pulled away from under his feet. Saul Street was Ray's first and only home, sold, most of its possessions disposed of without any thought or consideration for his memorable attachments and values. No consultation was had. No opinion was considered. No credence sought or given for how Ray might be feeling or what he might have wanted to keep.

Time heals. As we all adjust to being the lone parent family that we have become, living on Saul Road gradually wins over to provide a renewed comfort within our accepted new home. Even Ray appears at least superficially to adapt to the changes. Ray, by nature, needs stability and familiarisation. Stability in his physical surroundings, in his relationships with others, especially family, and in his daily routines. Without this stability, he has no familiarisation or routine upon which to anchor, no compass to mark his position or to guide his course for the day. Change or remove any element and Ray finds himself beyond his comfort zone and quickly becomes disorientated, confused and agitated. As we fail to recognise the impact of the compounding changes to his life, Ray's agitation festers and boils until the rage erupts, acting like a safety valve to vent what he can't articulate.

His time at secondary school comes to an end, change.

Mum arranges for Ray to attend the Thomas Doran Training Centre, change.

Relocated away from his home at Parkanaur, on the outskirts of Dungannon, change.

As a weekly boarder, change.

Change, change, change, change.

These changes to routine, school friends, surroundings, accommodation, family support, should have flashed warning signs in large neon lights. They probably did but we were all so self-absorbed that we couldn't or didn't see what was blindingly obvious. Poor Ray, his world is fragmenting and the rest of his family are too preoccupied to notice, to care. What a frightening, lonely path we put Ray on without even the most basic crutches to lean upon.

From the day that I screamed and chased Mum from the room I appoint myself as Ray's personal guardian, his counsellor and his mentor. Quite an ambitious job description for *Me*, a teenager. What I lack in professional qualifications or experience I compensate through unconditional love that grows into a lifelong devotion. Instinct screams at *Me* that Thomas Doran holds the key to more than just unhappiness at being estranged from his family as a weekly boarder. Despite my persistence or perhaps, more likely, my clumsy counselling inexperience, Ray keeps the source of his pain deeply buried within. Only in later years and only through patient and sensitive probing do I manage to peel back the layers of scar tissue that had formed to cover the infectious tumour who was, for, anonymity, I will call Billy Bates.

Billy bunked in the same room as Ray at Thomas Doran and quickly tagged Ray as an easy target for extorting money and sweets but also for gratifying his violent sadistic nature. Money and sweets were Ray's most valued possessions and, despite his soft nature, I can only imagine how strenuously he would have tried to hold onto both. Billy bullied and threatened behind the closed bedroom doors every Sunday evening upon arrival. The more Ray resisted the more the threats escalated into physical violence. The more Ray became accustomed to the violence and could hold out for a little longer, the more Billy increased the nature of his violence towards Ray. Thumps, punches and kicks became severe choking episodes. Sometimes launched on arrival and sometimes delayed until Ray, lulled into a false sense of security, had managed to fall asleep. Even after Billy had extorted every last penny and every last sweet, he continued to practise his physical and physiological torture for purely sadistic pleasure and self-gratification. Although I suspected that this gratuitous violence crossed other boundaries, I could never persuade Ray to fully reveal and acknowledge other suspected abuses. In a way, I understood some of his pain was so acute, so damaging to self-esteem, that it might be best left buried both for Ray and for *Me*, knowing that I was so ill-equipped to properly manage this form of suspected abuse if it came to the surface. Poor Ray lived with this weekly torment for three years. Teasing out some details of the story and exorcising his pain, took *Me* over three decades before I witnessed his trust in others fully restored.

My parallel life at this time could not be more different. I love my new school, Down High. I adore my wide and ever-growing circle of friends, particularly Jen, Sophie and Izzie who become my closest and most trusted accomplices in crime. Sophie teaches *Me* how to smoke cigarettes and look really 'cool' whilst inhaling, but inwardly turning green. Izzie teaches *Me* how to drink alcohol from Babycham to vodka without becoming sick, but if I am sick, how to discreetly hide and dispose of the evidence. Jen teaches *Me* how to feed my new vices by plundering small but regular quantities from the bar at her father's locally-owned hotel. We host girly pyjama sleep-over parties at each other's houses and spend Easter and summer school holidays together, visiting local beaches at Tyrella and Coney Island on the South Down coast, each a bike ride from home in Downpatrick. A time when, through rose-tinted sunglasses, the sun always seemed to shine in Ireland, before I reach sixteen years of age only to realise that it didn't. By fourteen I am old enough to be allowed to travel on an aeroplane for the very first time to discover Spain and over the next few years various islands in the Mediterranean as Jen's travelling companion with her parents. Boys feature but are never allowed to seriously threaten or disrupt 'our special girls only fraternity'. They do provide for great dramatic performances when anyone from our girly gang of four is hurt or even worse gets 'dumped' by any boy that temporarily manages to break through into our inner circle. We are total divas. Fashion, make-up, music and dancing. What more could a girl want or need in life?

Doe pursues a more sober and sensible lifestyle with her own gang, whose inner circle comprises Dixie, Maddie and Elsie. Doe gets *Me* an invite to hang out with her gang for a weekend of fun down on Dixie's family farm. Cleaning and preparing dirty vegetables straight from the farm fields. Baking in the large farmhouse kitchen with a strong prevailing smell of manure permeating everywhere that instantly kills any appetite I might have worked up for eating what we baked. Cleaning the cattle feeding troughs, riding horses before cleaning out their hay sheds, and then relaxing in the evening learning how to sew, cross-stitch and crochet. What amazing fun Doe has, absolutely not, *Me* thinks. I decide to keep to my own company from now on and presume that Doe probably wouldn't want to spend an exchange weekend hanging out with my friends.

Shortly before Doe's fifteen birthday, Uncle Robert and Auntie Edith pay us a visit from their home in Somerset. I pay little attention to their visit as they spent hours talking to Mum and Doe whilst drinking gallons of tea. At the end of their day-long conference, Mum looks sad and teary but Doe is hopping, skipping and dancing. Over the next two weeks Mum spends a lot of time fussing around Doe, buying her new clothes and shoes and a large travelling suitcase. I pick up bits of conversation and piece together that Doe is going over to Somerset to stay with Uncle Robert and Auntie Edith 'for a while'. Lucky Doe, off on a holiday to Somerset; when I'm older I'll get to go to Somerset by myself too, I reasoned.

About two weeks later the day arrives for Doe to leave and Doe, Ray and *Me* are excitedly chatting and chirping like little canaries. We all tumble from the house and into the car, with Mum last to get into the driver's seat for the journey to the airport to enable Doe to catch her flight to Bristol. The conversation in the back of the car speculates on all the exciting places that Doe will get to visit in Somerset and the big house where Doe will stay with Uncle Robert and Auntie Edith, located on the boundary of a small village between Bridgwater and Glastonbury. Just before we arrive at the airport I ask Doe, *when will we be picking you up again?*

I don't know but I hope I can come back to see you all at Christmas, she replies, looking earnest. Laughing at her joke I play along, *as if school will let you miss that much time for a holiday.* With a very serious tone Doe drops the bombshell, *I'm not joking; I'm starting to train as a nurse and I don't know when or how often I will be able to come home to see you all.* I spin around to look at Mum and know Doe is telling the truth as Mum can barely drive for the tears now running down both cheeks. As the four of us pull into the airport parking bay we must have looked pitiful all bawling and crying and incapable of talking in sentences. Staying in the car while Mum escorts Doe into the airport, Ray and *Me* sit in the back seat, holding hands and sobbing. We can no longer again sing 'Doe, Ray *Me*'.

After Doe has left, Mum seems to withdraw more and more and with Ray continuing to board at Thomas Doran, I find myself assuming the role that Doe used to fulfil, cooking, ironing and cleaning. Never as good as Doe but I manage to keep a semblance of normality going within the house, at least for the appearance of any outsiders that might call. But even they seem to have become fewer and fewer.

Over the next couple of years, I feel schizophrenic. During the day at school, happy and normal, but on weeknights lonely and increasingly depressed, whiling away repetitive evenings by listening to my favourite Dr Hook songs over and over again. Yearning for every approaching weekend, I try to capture a lost feeling of being truly alive by organising or attending a house party on as many Friday and Saturday evenings as possible. I resent Doe for deserting us. For deserting *Me* and leaving *Me* to pick up all the pieces. I resent Mum for being here physically but always appearing to be absent. I miss Ray for being at Thomas Doran. I am racked with guilt for my selfishness at weekends, deserting poor Ray continually after I promised to always be there for him, but I need to escape. I need to vent my own steam, to burn off energy, to capture that *life in abundance* that I was promised after Daddy's 'departure'. Going into my sixteenth year I know that I must settle down to study for my GCSE examinations but the mischievous voice that whispers into my ear undermines my attempts to be mature and responsible. Chipping away with suggestive questions, study for what, for why, how? Mum's behaviour is now more and more erratic and argumentative. *How the hell can anyone concentrate in this madhouse*, I concur with my inner voice. I try to socialise even more, putting each of my friends under inexcusable pressure to accompany *Me* to the pub for a drink after school, on weeknights, at weekends, any excuse to reduce my time at home. One by one they all begin to make excuses.

I can't, I need to study.
You can study tomorrow night, I reply.
My parents won't give me the money.
I'll get my Mum to give Me more money, I counter.
I can't, I need to go to bed early… I need to dye my hair tonight… I need to help my parents with the gardening this evening…

Look it's all right for you, you can do what you want. Just because your Mum is an alcoholic and doesn't care what you get up to, finally blurts Sophie with her usual naive honesty. *My parents say that you get what you want when you want it to keep you out of your Mum's way so that she can drink.*

I know that Mum takes a drink now and again, but she never touched the stuff when Daddy was alive. He liked an occasional drink but he always kept the bottles locked away. Locked away from us – Doe, Ray and *Me* – so that we didn't drink it by mistake. That makes sense. Well it did then. Mum does drink a bit now, gin and orange, one or two most nights *to help her unwind, to sleep*, she claims. Nothing wrong with that, some people take sleeping pills. That doesn't make her an alcoholic. Old Sammy in town, he's an alcoholic, dirty, smelly, stinking of beer. Mum's nothing like Sammy. Mum's clean and well-dressed and, a woman. Alcoholics are old men not young women. Not my Mum.

After losing most of the following night's sleep, tossing and turning, as much in my mind as in my bed, I try to push the thoughts from my head to concentrate on school. I need to sit my maths examination today and I'm rubbish at maths... I can never get things to add up properly. Mum's not an alcoholic, it doesn't add up.

After school, I go straight home. I'm so sure I have failed the exam but I'm going to make Mum and *Me* a lovely tea. Steak and potatoes, Mum's favourite. Mum's not home so I get started and by six o'clock I have everything ready to plate. Mum arrives shortly after and I greet her coming through the front door with a cheery call from the kitchen, *Mum I've made tea, steak and potatoes, it's all ready, come and eat.*

I'm not hungry, I'm just thirsty. I'll make myself a drink.

No need, I have some juice on the table, come into the kitchen.

Standing in the kitchen door frame Mum explodes, *Damn it I told you I'm not hungry. I just want a drink.*

You don't need that drink, look I've got juice here, come and sit with Me, pour that down the sink and come and eat.

Are you bloody deaf? she screams. *If I want a drink I'll have a drink and it's none of your dammed business.*

End of discussion. Mum retreats into the living room for a top-up. I can hear the bottle clinking against her now empty glass.

Furious, I lift the frying pan that is keeping the steak warm and toss both pan and steak into the swing bin below the kitchen sink followed by the saucepan with the boiled potatoes. Storming off to my bedroom I slam the door behind *Me*. Suddenly exhausted, I collapse on top of my bed. Defeated, hungry, confused and seething with anger and frustration I start to cry. I can't stop crying. My Mum is an alcoholic. The realisation that all my friends appeared to have known what I could not see for myself is devastating. *How could I be so blind, so stupid, so selfish?*

An uneasy truce settles between Mum and *Me* following our exchange that allows *Me* to attempt to resume my revision enough to sit my final examination test papers. Remarkably I manage to successfully pass six General Certificate of Secondary Education, GCSE, Ordinary or O-Levels. Not great grades but passes, the highest grade for Domestic Science, so I mustn't be too bad at cooking. Encouraged by Ray returning home in June, having finished his term and time at Thomas Doran, my spirits lift for the summer ahead. I busy myself helping more around the house and spending time with Ray who seems quieter and more distant since his return. Mum appears to be drinking less, certainly less obviously in front of Ray and *Me*, controlling her gin and orange to perhaps one or two a week in the quieter time before bed. Thank goodness, as Mum is spending a lot of time driving back and forth to Portadown visiting Uncle Jimmy and Granny Sarah.

Portadown seems to be having some effect as Mum appears more focused, determined, and happier than I have seen her for months. One Saturday morning in early July, Mum asks Ray and *Me* to come with her to Portadown, *I have something that I want to show you both*. Not knowing what Mum has in mind but shored up by her obvious excitement, we set off around ten in the morning. We travel the tedious journey through Ballynahinch, the long tortuous road up and down through the rolling drumlins to Dromore, into Lurgan, eventually reaching Portadown around eleven thirty; a journey that is to be repeated many times over the next two months.

Knowing from previous trips where Uncle Jimmy lives, a small detached bungalow bought for him by Mum after Daddy died, I'm slightly confused as we drive to the opposite side of town turning into a small cul-de-sac of chalet-style semi-detached houses on a hill behind Craigavon Area Hospital. Pulling up outside number 25, Mum declares with some obvious pride and enthusiasm, *I've bought this house.*

Why have you bought a house in Portadown, is Uncle Jimmy moving? I ask.

No, we're moving, you, me and Ray.

What, when, why, a hundred questions fly into my mind causing complete turmoil as I think about my life in Downpatrick, my friends, my school, everything. I know nothing about Portadown except that it's where Uncle Jimmy, Uncle Freddie, Auntie Ethel and Granny Sarah live. Mum, oblivious to my sudden hysteria continues talking calmly over all my protests as if this is a decision previously discussed amongst the three of us and consensually agreed. She simply states as a matter of fact, *well it's done, we're moving, everything's organised and Granny is moving in with us to help…*

I'm sixteen, my whole life exists in Downpatrick, I can't just close it down and start again but it seems Mum can, is going to and just has.

If you 'choose the life you lead', why do I suddenly feel that for *Me*, 'I have no choice'?

> *Heaven knows we need never be ashamed of our tears, for they are rain upon the blinding dust of earth, overlying our hard hearts. I was better after I had cried, than before – more sorry, more aware of my own ingratitude, more gentle.*
>
> Charles Dickens, Great Expectations

Chapter 5

The fire that scorched *Me*

Sometimes God will deliver you from the fire. Other times God will make you fireproof and take you through the fire.

Joel Osteen

Aaah, I hate it… hate it… hate it.
Our new house.
Portadown.
The people who live here.
I hate it all. Mum has no right to do this to *Me*. She hates *Me*. Why else would she be so cruel to even think that I could be happy to leave my home, my town, my friends, at sixteen years of age, and for no good reason. I hate her too. Ray hates it here too; I haven't actually asked him but I'm sure that he does. He must. And Granny, propped up in an armchair in the corner of the lounge, like an over-stuffed mannequin dressed with layers of clothing and covered with blankets. Never moving from breakfast-time until supper and then back to bed. Just sits and prays and wets herself. Although into her nineties she used to be surprisingly independent, washing and feeding herself, moving around her own house, washing and ironing her own clothes. At least she was when

living in her own home, but since moving in with us she does absolutely nothing. Just sits and prays and pees.

I'm behaving much as any teenager might if whisked away from their best friends to be plunged into the murky uncharted waters of a new town and new school. I look for fault in everything and everyone. It proves easy to find. I become obsessed with how badly the local kids speak and behave. One of Daddy's legacies was to ensure that we received the best that education could offer, to speak properly and clearly and to behave respectfully and in a dignified manner when in public. I find myself surrounded by teenagers that are lazy in their speech, substituting the word '*like*' to compensate for failing to think of an appropriate word to construct their sentences. *Like I went to town like to meet like my friend like in Port-e-down*. The knockout punch being to finish each sentence with the expression '*you know*'. No I don't know, so why don't you explain it to *Me* properly, I feel *like* screaming. God, even I have caught the *like* speech bug. Maybe it's the accent but I shy away from conversations, finding the tone and delivery unnecessarily aggressive and confrontational. It seems to *Me* that if found guilty of an alternative view you risk being threatened with '*having your pan knocked in*' or '*your lights knocked out*'. Either way, in or out, the options sounded very bleak.

My self-pitying reflections are interrupted by some counter-judgements levelled against *Me*. Comments made some years beyond my present reflective time sequence cut across my memory frame, creating an alternative perspective that challenges my jaundiced view towards arriving in Portadown. Kevin, a cousin of my then future husband, after listening curiously to *Me* procrastinating, chastens *Me* by characterising *Me* as a '*pretentious snob*'. *Me*, a snob and a pretentious snob to boot, surely not. Then I'm reminded of Nick, T's uncle, who delights in affectionately mocking *Me* for repeatedly rolling out my favoured expression '*golly gosh*

I'm mortified' every time I'm caught or exposed by my own shortcomings or mistakes. Arguing with myself I concede, looking back, perhaps *Me* is a little snobby and just a touch pretentious as I arrive in Portadown as a sixteen-year-old.

Recognising that I have another choice to make, to continue to wallow in self-pity or to adopt some advice scripted by my classic film idol Bette Davis when faced with challenging or daunting scenarios. I opt for the latter. *Get the war paint on, get dressed to impress and get back out there.*

Mum directs *Me* to complete my education in Lurgan, a town five miles from Portadown, enrolling *Me* in a secretarial course that I absolutely despise. After the first month, I persuade my year group teacher to allow *Me* to switch to continue my studies through conventional A-level courses. By exercising my own right to choose, this change in direction puts *Me* directly on a collision course with my future husband and soul mate T.

T finds himself banished from Portadown, estranged too from his friends to salvage some educational credibility in Lurgan, having flunked most of his O-level examinations. His excuse, distracted by the opportunity to travel extensively across Europe in the heatwave summer of '76. As he later jokes, *I had my choices too. To study or to earn money to travel. I chose the short-term excitement to explore Europe for one summer, over the longer-term potential to explore the world perpetually had I only focused more on my education. Don't compromise your future by paying too high a price for the present*, became his guiding mantra.

The bus journey to and from Lurgan for school is the most tedious journey imaginable. The person who designed the new 'city' of Craigavon that straddles the older, more settled towns of Portadown and Lurgan clearly had an unhealthy obsession with roundabouts. The short five-mile journey lasts more than an hour going around and around in circles to access virtually every newly-developed housing estate en route, with rarely any new passengers actually catching the bus between the two town stops. A few months into this daily merry-go-round to and from school, I notice a boy around my age taking the same journey, although he is already on the bus before my collection and continues to a stop beyond my return. I'm aware that he looks at *Me* furtively when he thinks I'm distracted, reading or looking aimlessly through the side windows. I catch his gaze in the reflection from the glass, watching him watching *Me*, but he doesn't speak. The boy attends the same school, although I have only recently noticed him since becoming aware that he travels the same route daily. One morning during break-time, this boy approaches *Me* in the girls' locker area, against school rules, causing an excited stir amongst the other girls. *I've seen you on the bus and would really like to sit with you. I love your style, can't miss you with your green coat. We could talk and get to know each other.* Not exactly a blow *Me* away chat-up line. I'm furious that he has singled *Me* out in front of the small gathering of giggling girls, but slightly flattered to be the centre of attention. *If you like, I can't stop you sitting where you want on the bus,* I reply playing it cool. *Great I'll see you on the bus after school,* he declares with a beaming smile and is gone. Arrogant, self-confident twit I think, but I find myself smiling too.

The Chinese whispers spread that I've been asked out across my year group and soon everyone wants to offer their opinion. *Be careful he's a player. He thinks he's God's gift to girls.* Rather than putting *Me* off I find myself more intrigued; I'll play him along and have some fun. After school, I catch the bus as usual but there is no sign of the boy. I shrug my shoulders and think that he has bottled it, so much for 'Mr Self-confident'. Just as the bus is about to pull away from the town centre stop, T waves to the driver and hops quickly onto the bus looking flustered and out of breath. Walking down the aisle to where I am seated two rows from the back, he shuffles into the outside seat and says *Hi*. *Hi* I reply, noticing for the first time his sun-tanned complexion, dark hair and amazing teeth. You are quite attractive and I find myself smiling and blushing. The conversation flows easily and I realise that rather than arrogantly confident and self-assured, T is quite shy but easy to talk with and interesting. For the first time, the journey home passes too quickly and I am surprised to find myself excitedly looking forward to the journey tomorrow. After a couple of weeks, T leaves the bus at my stop to walk *Me* home before continuing by foot the extra mile to his own home. I have found a friend in Portadown at last, a good friend, now my boyfriend.

T meets my family, Mum, Ray and Gran and brings a new light into my dark world as gradually we become inseparable. My social life is revived as we go to dances and discos, to the cinema or to the newly opened first Chinese restaurant to arrive in Portadown. Somewhere along the way we fall in love and I discover that Portadown isn't such a bad place to live after all. School is bearable, I pick up a part-time job at the local hotel as a receptionist, and Ray secures a place at a local day centre and appears happier too. Poor Ray, for months after moving he has no escape from home and spends his days lining his saved coins up in neat rows on the lounge table. Counting his total, Ray records each pound saved as a pencil line, five pounds drawn as four parallel vertical lines with a fifth horizontal line scored through the neat vertical lines. Much like a prisoner marking the days served until his release.

Since moving, Mum has sunk more deeply into her dependency on gin and orange, stumbling from one drunken day to the next. If not topping up her 'anaesthetic' to numb the pain, despair and loneliness of her life, Mum chokes herself and those around her chain-smoking thirty Silk Cut Lights a day. A toxic fog hovers to stain and stale our house and lives, exacerbating Ray's asthma and necessitating more frequent nebulising to control his breathing. The unpredictability of her mood swings plays havoc on our nerves. Never knowing whether we are going to find the soft, gentle, contrite, remorseful Mum promising to sort herself out, or the manipulative, nasty, vindictive and spiteful Mum that torments us for hours with her vile language and sarcastic put-downs. Each of us, Ray, Gran and *Me* learn to survive Mum's tornado effect, when she swoops down upon one or all of us from a clear sky to wreak sudden chaos and misery upon our lives, disappearing as suddenly as she arrived, leaving *Me to* clear the resultant mess and collateral damage.

Ray characteristically soaks up the punishment, absorbing each verbal punch until Mum's energy finally dissipates in the face of no reaction. Gran scowls and mutters incoherently to herself and then provokes greater abuse by praying more fervently for Mum's soul and salvation. *Me*, I am learning to ignore the provocations, by feigning apathy, laughing or agreeing. Any reverse psychology that gives Mum the perception that she has won the reaction sought rather than rising to the provocation and swallowing the bait cast into my face. I discover that it's impossible to rationally win any verbal argument with a drunk. It simply pours more alcohol onto the fire rapidly fuelling a twisted or belligerent throwaway comment into a raging inferno. Better to defuse the inevitable flare-up with a soothing or phoney submissive or lied agreement, designed to confound and confuse her expectation for a more argued response.

Increasingly, the little weevil undertaker Morris has become a frequent visitor. Always arriving on a Saturday and at times more destructively midweek, as I arrive home to find Mum the worse for wear after a day's drinking. Cleverly worming his way into Mum's life by providing a false escape, inevitably only as far as the nearest pub where he can manipulate Mum's underlying nature to generously sponsor any good cause, even if it's only a new pair of shoes or clothing. Smug, devious and calculating, I am no match for this leech as he establishes himself as Mum's indispensable crutch. Does he now want to gloat that he buried Charlie and both his wives I speculate?

Torn by conflicting loyalties and emotions, I can't continue to fight on so many fronts. To protect Mum from herself and against the malicious intents of Morris, to shield Ray from the worst effects of Mum and Morris and to protect Granny from what she sees as 'the evils of drink'. I resign myself to handing out sticking plasters of comforting words of assurance to Ray and Granny and allow Mum and Morris to pursue their destructive journey together. Thank God I have T, my escape, my sanity, my confidant. I cannot fully hide the shame and embarrassment that Mum causes. T sympathises and says that he understands, but, how can he? His parents don't drink; T can try to understand but has no idea of the reality behind our closed curtains. For his sake and mine, I work hard to keep it this way, to protect T and *Me* from the worst excesses of Mum.

I pass my driving test first time and six months ahead of T, a blow to his male ego. Mum insures *Me* to drive her car, a great independence but at a cost; I can drive to the off-sales to replenish her supply of 'anaesthetic', as I now call it. I feel a total hypocrite; I hate feeding Mum's addiction but the freedom to escape is an alluring respite that I come to depend upon. Shortly afterwards, T secures his driver's licence, first time too and so, ego duly restored, he takes *Me* to Omeath, a small village across the border about seven miles into the south of Ireland on the shores of Carlingford Lough.

We spend a beautiful afternoon walking along the shoreline, talking and dreaming about our future together and, before leaving for home, we drop into a small café on the main road through the village to have something to eat. Sitting at the table by the window, I gaze at the local kids playing without a care on the street outside and feel an overwhelming happiness. I feel light-headed, T's voice fades into the distance as I slide into unconsciousness from the wooden chair onto the linoleum flooring.

Gradually, the sound of T's voice breaks through my fuzziness with a concern that forces *Me* to focus. I know I didn't fall off my chair and yet, I can see that I am lying crumbled on the dirty floor between my chair and the glass window. *I think you fainted, it's probably the heat and hunger,* is Dr T's diagnosis. I laugh, more to mask my embarrassment from the waitress staring at *Me* from the counter and retake my seat. T smiles and I feel stupid but safe with T.

> *And that fire inside you, it can be turned into a negative form or a positive form. And I gradually realised that I had this fire and that it had to be used in a positive way.*
>
> John Newcombe

Chapter 6

Out of the fire and into the frying pan for *Me*

Out of suffering have emerged the strongest souls; the most massive characters are seared with scars.

Kahlil Gibran

Life has settled into a comfortable pattern of dull routine disrupted occasionally by Mum irrationally demanding, arguing or huffing over what, I am never quite sure. I have long mastered the art of functioning quite normally whilst managing Mum's eccentricities, much as you would an irritating bluebottle circling the room as you work. If the fly comes too close, you flinch at the threatening buzz that alarms your hearing, prompting a verbal outburst or a retaliatory hand swipe to ward off any further annoyance. After a while you learn to coexist with the constant background buzzing of the bluebottle, ironically finding yourself stopping, listening and worrying when there is an unnatural silence in the room.

My final A-Level examinations are fast approaching and, buoyed by the results from my mock trials earlier before Easter, I discover a new self-confidence and determination. Thinking positively to convince myself that I can complete my finals, that I can achieve good grades, I fantasise that university could, just might, be possible. I struggle not to dwell too much on this fantasy, fearing that it will distract my focus on study and revision or, worse still, it might prove to be just an illusionary bubble that bursts and evaporates into mist, just as my fingers reach out to touch the dream.

Experience has cautioned *Me* not to step beyond the moment but to concentrate on the here and now, to be happy and content in the peace that reigns within the realm of dull reality. Old Morris has been absent for a couple of weeks due to illness and the atmosphere around the house feels noticeably more relaxed and, normal. Even Mum appears to have embraced a run of sobriety taking responsibility and control for managing the house a bit more, allowing *Me* the space to actually follow a study plan. *Me* following a plan, any plan seems strangely alien living in an environment of unpredictability that at times can escalate into near chaos. Despite my tendency to seek any escapism from the house, I find myself unexpectedly drawn to an unfamiliar quiet and calm that accompanies Mum's sobriety. I am almost spellbound by the lack of excitement that follows. An absence of unpredictability and tension has descended upon the house. I feel myself drunk with the dullness of going through a whole day without an argument, a worry or a weighted sense of responsibility towards Ray or Granny.

Monday morning and I am feeling a little off colour, just a head cold, but excuse enough for *Me* to self-justify a day off school to revise at home. The sun is shining, Ray and Granny are up, dressed, fed and settled in the lounge. Mum is preparing to go into town to shop, sober, so my chauffeuring skills are redundant for the day. I spend the morning studying in my bedroom hardly noticing the hours drifting towards midday with the absence of any interruptions and the quietness of the house. As my eyes tire with the strain of reading, I become acutely aware of the rumble of hunger in my stomach deciding now is a good time to take a break and to see what is in the fridge for lunch. With Mum in her bedroom applying make-up ahead of going to town, I offer to make lunch and prance down the stairs humming and singing with a contentment that makes *Me* think life is good.

Mum has left lunch prepped, my favourite lamb chops, with the potatoes peeled and 'chipped' for frying. I turn the ceramic hob settings for both rings on the cooker up to the maximum six setting and in no time the chops are lightly fried and the chips beautifully deep fat fried, lightly browned and crisp. As I plate up for Mum, Ray, Granny and *Me*, I see a chicken leg on the side bench that has been left over from the Sunday roast. Taught never to waste good food I return the chip pan, just a saucepan with a frying basket that conveniently fits, back onto the hob, turning the setting again to the maximum six setting and pop the chicken leg into the hot oil before diverting my attention towards garnishing lunch with peas boiled in the microwave. As Ray loves chicken, much more than lamb, I cut his chop in two dividing it between Mum and *Me* and turn away from the table to retrieve the pre-cooked chicken from the bubbling fryer.

Standing by the cooker while waiting for the chicken to reheat for a few more moments, my giddy mood explodes into light-headed confusion as I stumble forward, losing balance but managing to grasp the cooker edges with both hands to steady myself. My mind is blank, incapable of holding thoughts or controlling actions as my eyes roll upwards, losing focus, disorientating *Me*. I can smell the hot cooking oil close to my face just as my legs buckle, forcing my knees to collide with the oven door as my head and shoulders recoil backwards, as if in slow motion, but instantly and spasmodically. My arms flail upwards. I defensively reach for a new anchor causing the loose sleeve of my mohair cardigan to snag the wire frying basket just as my legs crumble beneath

Me. My head flails back, crashing directly onto the kitchen floor.

A searing pain, unimaginable in intensity plunges *Me* into darkness.

Emerging from my blindness I hear voices, shouting, confusing *Me*, familiar sounding, but the voices of strangers.

Opening my eyes, I frantically scan the misty emptiness for any recognition. Following the voice to my left, through watering eyes, I barely recognise Granny shouting and praying. *God help her, God help her.* My head flops to the right, blinking and blinking, Ray comes into fuzzy focus looking pale, almost ashen as death, staring, his mouth agape, eyes wide, glaring at *Me* terrified. Darkness overwhelms *Me* again. Through the inky blackness that muddles my thoughts I pick up random words. Mum is shouting hysterically. I recognise the calming but assertive voice of Liz, a neighbour, taking control, instructing Mum to be quiet. *Don't touch, leave her clothes, where's the ambulance? You are going to be okay dear, everything will be fine, hold my hand.* Darkness.

This will help… just feel a small pin prick in your arm. My body is on fire with every nerve scorching my skin but I feel cold, freezing cold. I know I'm trembling, my body is jerking with the intensity of the cold but I can't control myself. I hear Liz, *listen to the ambulance man… hospital… just going to give you an injection… pain… help you…* A warm sensation begins to creep through *Me*, the darkness overwhelms *Me* again.

The light hurts my eyes. I will myself to turn my head sideways to escape the penetrating light. White coats, blue uniforms, talking, walking, in, out and beyond my vision. My head rolls to rest my cheek on a pillow and I can hear a new voice, an older voice, male, authoritatively diminishing all other voices to quietening whispers. *I need to assess the damage* he tells *Me* with comforting assurance. *I am going to prick you with this needle to see where it hurts and where it doesn't. You're a very brave girl. I'll be as quick as I can.*

How can I feel his needle when my body is screaming at *Me* from every direction?

Watching his hand, anticipating a sharp pain as the needle held between his thumb and finger goes down. Nothing, down, nothing, down again and I try to scream but only a gagging noise comes from the back of my throat. *Sorry* he apologises. I turn my head, stare up at the lights, like visiting the dentist, and ignore the pain. My throat hurts, dry and hard to swallow. *Aaah, sorry* he repeats.

What time is it I croak? *Welcome back young lady, its eleven thirty and it's a lovely Wednesday morning.* You mean eleven thirty Monday night I contradict the nurse. *No, you have slept really well, it's Wednesday morning. I'll let the doctor know that you are awake. He would like to talk with you.* As the nurse leaves the room I try to understand where I am, what has happened to *Me*. I know that I'm in hospital, I recognise the nurse's uniform. Bandaged up like an Egyptian mummy I struggle to move. Tubes are connected to my arms. I follow the tube from my right arm to see it attached to a fluid drip. Turning my head, I follow the tube coming from my left arm and realise that it is not a tube but a wire connected to a machine. The machine resonates a monotonous bleep, bleep, bleep.

The nurse comes back into the room followed by a doctor. I assume a doctor by his white coat. He smiles and I find that I can't help but smile back at him. *You've been in the wars*, he says and then reacting to my obvious confused look he corrects himself and with a more serious tone informing *Me* that I have *been in an accident. Do you remember having an accident?* he asks *Me*. I shake my head, *no* I croak, my eyes go misty and a tear trickles down my cheek. I feel stupid, I don't know what my accident was, so why am I crying.

You have been badly burned. We have stabilised your burns but you have lost a lot of fluids and I need you to stay on antibiotics for a few days. Burns, how? The chip pan, my mind is racing. *After your wounds have settled, the plastic surgeon will assess how we can improve…* I don't understand, plastic, wounds, damage. *We'll talk more later in the week; the nurses will change your dressings and you can get some more rest.* And he's gone.

Mum visits *Me* in the afternoon, she looks wretched, tired and pale without make-up. I hope she hasn't been drinking. Liz follows Mum into the room, a side ward I have determined. Liz, her usual bright, jolly self, bounds over to the bed greeting *Me* with a big kiss to my forehead. *How are you today sweetheart?* she asks. I start to whimper, *what happened to Me?*

Liz gently informs *Me* that I *have had an accident*. The chip pan fell on *Me* and that I was burnt by the hot oil. *How?* I ask. *We don't know. You somehow managed to stumble to the lounge and collapsed onto the couch. Your Mum ran for help and we called for an ambulance. Fortunately, the hospital is close and you were taken to A&E immediately. How bad is it?* I ask looking directly at Liz. *I don't know. The doctors will talk to you. You are in the best place and they will do everything they can. You stay brave, we are all praying for your recovery,* Liz assures *Me* with such conviction and I believe her. I look to Mum; she's nodding but I can see the tears brimming up in her eyes.

Over the next couple of days, I am overwhelmed with nurses, doctors and consultants.

Some talk to *Me* about what led to the accident. My fainting, *has this happened before, when, how often?* Others concentrate on my immediate treatment explaining the differences between first, second and third degree burns. It seems I have succumbed to all three. First degree burns are the most superficial, painful but shallow surface burns that heal and should leave no marks or scars. I have several first degree, splashes from the hot oil, mostly to exposed skin further away from the main point of impact. Second degree are deeper, causing slightly more damage: *they hurt the most, blister very badly but the pain is good* says the doctor, *if you can feel pain the burn is deep but not so deep that it has damaged your nerves*. I'm glad he thinks second degree is good, I think they hurt like hell. Third degree burns are the deepest, probably caused by the highest concentration of hot oil '*pooling*' on my body when I fell, the oil continuing to burn deep down into my skin with nowhere else to run off too. The burn penetrates so deep that it destroys the underlying sensory nerves within the tissue. You can't feel as much pain as with second degree but they are more serious and risk greater infection, take longer to treat and recover and can lead to longer term or permanent problems, particularly if the muscle around the joints is also damaged.

The doctors explain that I have over ten per cent second and third degree burns damage across my upper chest, right breast and right arm, a high and potentially life-threatening percentage. I have second degree burns around my lower neck and in areas of my upper and lower chest and a small number of first degree, secondary splash-back burns on my chin and lower arms. The mohair cardigan and light cotton blouse underneath afforded no protection against the scalding hot oil that poured onto my upper torso. My legs were protected by my denim jeans reducing the volume of penetrating oil to hit or reach my legs.

I dread the daily changing of bandages. Each time I am propped forward in the bed as the nurses very slowly and gently unravel the layers of white bandages. Below the bandages is a film of gauzed material covering the affected burns area making my skin feel as if it is being peeled off every time they remove this protective coating. Before the nurses apply a fresh treatment of a soothing lotion designed to keep the affected area moist and free from infection, a doctor seems to magically appear to test and retest the degree of burns within each affected area. I feel like a pin cushion as they prick their needles into every white blister and every blotch of red raw flesh designed to tell them which burn patches are recovering and to map the critical areas of third degree burns. *Pain is good*; try telling that to this voodoo doll.

My third group of devotees are the consultants. The *big cheeses* as the nurses call them. Tweedledum and Tweedledee as I inwardly think of them. In they come, they look, they grunt, they mutter to themselves or to each other and as I wait and look expectantly for their lofty conclusions, they simply pronounce *good*, and leave the room. I guess it could be worse if they concluded fine, okay or bad. It's good to be good, I reason, and look forward to their next enthralling visit.

My fainting causes concern with a couple of repeat episodes witnessed by the nurses. Blood tests have ruled out low sugar levels or diabetes so the consultant neurologist decides to run an electrocardiogram or ECG to test my heart which also proves to be a *non-contributing factor*, so resorts to authorising an electroencephalogram or EEG and scans to gather information for a diagnosis. The tests are inconclusive and neither confirm nor rule out epilepsy. It seems that I simply need to wait to see if my fainting persists and to monitor the conditions that precede any recurrence. Although not definitive, the neurologist alludes to stress. *The stress of exams and a typical teenager lifestyle* he pronounces with an air of diagnostic certainty. *That doesn't explain the first time I fainted in the café at Omeath* I cross-examine. I have my own suspicions that the stress of worrying about Mum's lifestyle is by far a greater source of stress, but loyalty to Mum censors *Me* from raising this as a contributory factor. *Mmmm, quite* he concedes and departs with a defeated frown.

Gradually, as my first week hospitalised nears to an end, I find myself cheered by the optimistic noises expressed by the treatment teams. I have got to know the nurses and we chat and joke and the day passes reasonably quickly. The doctors seem to have run short of needles and now only ambush *Me* by surprise with random visits and only to test smaller and more isolated areas. I guess the other areas are considered *good*. The consultant plastic surgeon introduces himself and talks *Me* through the skin grafting procedures that he has in mind for *Me*. Encouraged that this consultant can converse with more than single syllable words, I really warm to Mr Plastics, my new consultant with his patient and plain English explanations, encouraging my confidence with his determination to *make you (Me) as good as new again*. Despite the pain and discomfort and the total embarrassment caused by so many trainee doctors queuing up to look at my upper body burns, my spirits are lifted by Mr Plastics' optimism and assurance. He makes everything seem so simple to make *Me as good as new again*. We just take a little bit of skin from here and there to graft onto my third degree burn areas.

T begins to visit more often, now that the risk of infection is strictly controlled and the value of visitors cannot be underestimated to *help my morale* says the lead nurse. The first time T visits I panic; what will he think, how will he react to seeing *Me* like this? I should have known better. T walks straight up to my bed, kisses *Me* on the lips and tells *Me* I look great. *Liar*, but it feels good to hear it. My good school friend Tiana visits too and brings *Me* a mad pink nightie with matching fluffy slippers to help *glam up this drab place*. I absolutely love the sentiment as it makes *Me* laugh for the first time in days, even if the opportunity to model them is practically non-existent.

The big day for my first skin grafting operation arrives early during my second week in hospital. The nurses prepare *Me* for the surgery ahead and keep my spirits high despite the gnawing hunger pains caused by my 'nil by mouth' imposed since nine o'clock the previous evening. At two in

BI-CENTENARY PLAQUE ERECTED

A plaque commemorating the founding of Down County Infirmary in 1767 in a house in Saul Street, is admired by (from left): Mr. M. N. Hayes, town clerk, Mr. J. S. Boyd, consultant surgeon Downe Hospital, and Mr. C. Thompson, who resides in the house. The plaque, provided by the Urban Council, was erected this week.

A plaque commemorating the founding of Down Infirmary in 1767 in Saul Street, Downpatrick. Charles Thompson is pictured on right.

Daddy in doorway of Black and White garage in Downpatrick

Doe (right), Ray, Me (left)

Daddy with Doe (centre), Ray and Me

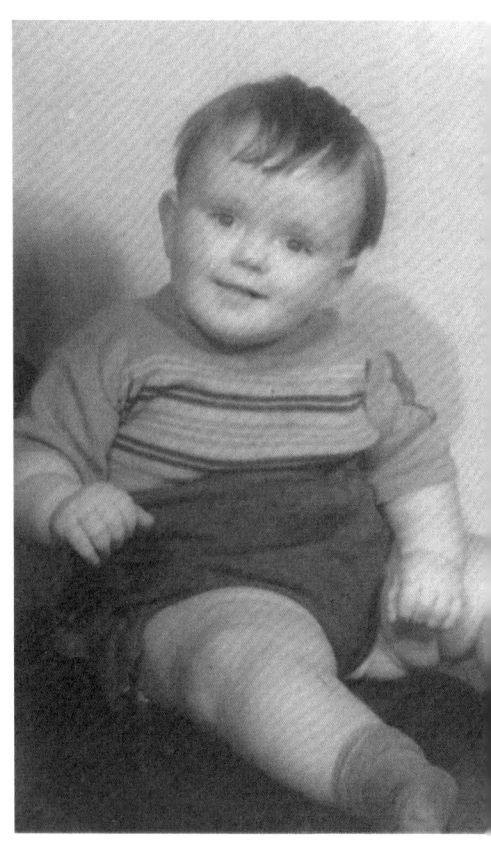

Left: Mummy and Daddy, my Christening
Right: Chubby toddler Ray

Doe Ray Me

Left: Doe and Me, choir members at Down Cathedral
Right: Ray laughing at my petulance

Me already showing impatience being made to wait outside a bar

Left: Ray using the lawnmower as a practice walking aid
Right: Moving forward as a lone parent family

Me, as a teenager taken just before my accident

Left: Ray and Me downcast at Doe leaving home
Right: Me experimenting with high collar fashion after my accident

Left: Granny at 99 years of age
Right: Uncle Jimmy with Andi

Ray meets his singing idol Daniel O'Donnell

Ray, propping up the bar at the Rovers Return

the afternoon my bed is wheeled from the room by a porter accompanied by one of my nurses to escort *Me* from the main ward to the lift for the descent to the operating theatre. My fear and apprehensions are allayed by the porter and nurse joking with each other and *Me* until I reach the theatre door, where I'm met by another scary nurse in green surgical gowns wearing a face mask. Her eyes smile at *Me* as I'm manoeuvred adjacent to and then transferred onto the operating table. The anaesthetist places a mask over my mouth and nose and asks *Me* to count backwards from ten. At seven I wake up feeling groggy and sore in the recovery ward.

Back on the ward I can't help but writhe with the new excruciating pains across my stomach and thighs. They are on fire, worse than the burns, constantly throbbing, pulsating with a numbing, aching pain that is inescapable, preventing no more than short exhaustive naps, but never a deep sleep. The next morning two nurses arrive to change the dressings on what they call my *donor* areas. This is my first opportunity to see what is causing the constant stinging sensation across my stomach and legs. As they pull back the bandages I cannot believe what I'm looking down upon. To *Me*, Mr Plastics has assaulted *Me*, sliced *Me* with an extra-wide potato scraper to peel layers of skin off my stomach and from the top of both of my thighs. My neck, upper body and right arm is burnt and now my stomach and legs are mutilated. For days, I have planned in my head how I will dress when it's time to leave hospital, how to cover my upper body but show a little flesh from my stomach and legs through higher waist tops and shorter skirts. Now I'm consigned to hide my whole body for life. It's so unfair.

My upper torso is encased within an elasticised vest, designed to iron out any ridges or wrinkles resulting from the skin grafting. The tightness is as suffocating as two hands grasped tightly around my throat with someone sitting heavily on my chest. The nurse stuns *Me* by casually declaring that I need to wear the vest for at least six months, perhaps a year. Seeing my reaction, she tries to reassure *Me* by concluding that when I *get used to the vest it won't feel quite so tight*. I don't want to get used to it, it's horrible and ugly. I feel that my spirit to fight on is being crippled and drained.

When you hit rock bottom there is only one way to go, up. Right?

Wrong, you can still go down further.

Mum visits daily. Earlier in my treatment I was glad of Mum's company as visitors were restricted to reduce the risk of infections. At times, I could smell that she had been drinking but was too tired and sore to face any fights or arguments. By the end of my second week in hospital my burns are settling and the grafts are responding well first time, reducing any need for possible repeat grafting. The donor areas, my belly and thighs, are becoming less painful but annoyingly itchy as the new skin pulls and knits into the wounds below and my spirits rise again, finding fun in the company of my nurses. Mum arrives, late, over thirty minutes into the afternoon visiting hour, looking dishevelled and the worse for drink. I see the furtive looks that the nurses give to each other and feel my frustration and rage rising but here is not the place to argue. We argue behind closed curtains, not in public. I desperately want to see Doe, to hear her voice, to talk to my big sister. I ask Mum could she not pay for Doe to fly home to visit *Me*? I miss her so much. I just need to talk to her. *No I can't*, Mum slurs. *I haven't told her that you hurt yourself.* She stumbles back from the bed, steadying herself by holding onto the visitor's chair. *Doe's sitting her nursing exams and I don't want you to upset her.*

You haven't told Doe that I nearly died. You think that I hurt… myself. You want to protect her from distress so that she can complete her exams in peace. You want to shield her from Me. Get out, get out! I scream. *Don't you ever come here again drunk. You're a disgrace, a total embarrassment to Me, to yourself. Get out!* I screech. For a second or two the vicious, nasty Mum-face looks set to retaliate but she doesn't. She glares at *Me* with undiluted contempt, makes a stupid snorting noise that is designed to demonstrate her disgust with *Me*, but what comes out of her mouth is a dribble of saliva oozing from the corner of her lips rather than the anticipated verbal bile. She turns and staggers from the room without another word. *See you tomorrow Mum* I sarcastically but wantonly call to the closing door.

Mum appears again, slipping in during afternoon visiting, five days after our spat and without a single reference to our argument, her absence, my health, nothing. Just pick up where we left off. Pretending to be sober but I can still smell the drink on her breath.

Somehow after the loneliness of the past five days it doesn't seem quite so important. I have a lot of thinking time in hospital. Drunk or sober, she is still my Mum.

> *One thing you can't hide – is when you're crippled inside.*
>
> John Lennon

Chapter 7

To have and to behold *Me*

A great marriage is not when the 'perfect couple' comes together.
It is when an imperfect couple learns to enjoy their differences.

Dave Meurer

After more than ten weeks cocooned in the sanctuary of my ward side room, today is the day for this wounded sparrow to be released back to what should be the security of its natural habitat, but more possibly back into the wild I fear. My time in hospital has evolved into a comforting routine with nurses, doctors and visitors each seducing *Me* with the flattery of being at the centre of everyone's care and attention. I find myself strangely hypnotised by the unfamiliar and yet totally alluring peace and quiet that dominates the periods between treatments. My fellow patients complain and lament the long hours spent shackled to their beds; to *Me* it seems refreshing and invigorating to simply sleep, think, eat, laugh. I feel a mental as well as a physical recovery strengthening *Me*, preparing *Me* for the challenges that inevitably lie ahead.

During the past days, I have mentally dressed and redressed myself, rehearsed what I might say and do as I prepare to be reunited with neighbours and friends whose lives have continued uninterrupted; prepping myself for my grand reappearance back into the real world, far beyond the asylum granted within my hospital room. My nervousness is all-consuming. How will I look, how will others look at *Me*, will they appreciate the seismic shift that has altered forever the landscape of my fashion choices? No longer trending for others to follow but now developing an individuality in fashion wear, sublimely designed to distract or mask from public exposure the scars that flare red and angry just below the neckline of my new wardrobe of patterned scarves and brightly-coloured polo necks.

   To celebrate the eve of my release, T pops back to visit around nine in the evening, explaining to the night nurses that he had left a book behind that he needs for the morning. Quietly entering the room, he raises his index finger to his lips, a signal for *Me* not to speak, gently closes the door and tiptoes over to my trolley table. From inside his black Crombie overcoat, T begins to extract a series of packages, each individually wrapped in brown Kraft paper. First, his inside right breast pocket reveals a foil container of fried rice. Switching to his inside left breast pocket emerges another foil container with the accompanying fried chicken with beansprouts. A magician on a roll he opens his coat to reveal a larger and deeper compartment discreetly sewn into the inside lining below the breast pocket that remarkably conceals an eight-inch diameter white dinner plate. I giggle at T's ingenuity to smuggle my favourite contraband into my prison cell past the watchful eyes of the ward guards. Barely controlling my obvious delight at this impromptu culinary treat, I feign a little disappointment by asking *what no chopsticks, surely you don't expect Me to eat with my magnificently-painted fingernails?* Looking deflated at my lack of enthusiasm or trust, T grins and, with a grand gesture, pulls a knife and fork wrapped in a paper tissue from his outside pocket. As the pièce de résistance, T furnishes a sachet of soy sauce from his top breast pocket. *Voilà* he declares. The noise of T's theatrics and my spontaneous applause attracts the uninvited attention of a ward nurse to our little party. The nurse gingerly opens the door, just wide enough to pop her head through the gap without flooding the outer ward with escaping light, quickly assesses what's happening and pretends to look shocked before smiling and quietly retreating, closing the door behind her. After weeks of hospital dinners, I'm in gastronomical heaven and demolish what truly tastes to *Me* a gourmet meal. T bids *Me* farewell with a goodnight kiss, whispering *I love you* before sneaking out of the ward a little after ten o'clock in the evening. I feel loved, secure and spoilt by T's most wonderful and unexpected treat, but more importantly completely distracted from fretting and worrying about tomorrow.

A little after two in the afternoon I am officially discharged from hospital. For stated *health and safety*, a porter escorts *Me* in a wheelchair to the hospital reception doors and waits silently with *Me*. Mum fetches the car, returning after what seems ages to park as close as possible under the canopy that extends over the revolving entrance doors. My senses are alive to the smell of the fresh easterly wind after the hot stale air that permeates the ward. The noises of passing traffic and people coming and going past my wheelchair sound amplified after the quietness of the ward, and my eyes squint with the brightness of natural sunlight after weeks of artificial lighting.

I feel strangely sad. My world has been surrounded by old and new friends twenty-four hours a day. Nurses and doctors interspersed between visiting friends and relatives. Patients, mostly transient, entering and leaving my closeted world, mostly within a few days or weeks, but some occasional longer stays as they recuperate from their own life-changing or life-limiting illnesses or accidents. I suddenly realise that I will miss them all, ships that pass in the night but each seeking safe anchorage in the company of fellow travellers.

Arriving home brings its own mixed emotions. Part of *Me* feels safe and comforted by familiar surroundings. Another part of *Me* scared, almost terrified, as I prepare to confront the crime scene where the remaining innocence of my youth was so violently assaulted. The absence of any welcoming home friends feels anticlimactic and yet paradoxically a party would be my worst nightmare. I quietly slip into the house seeking immediate refuge in my bedroom, taking comfort from recognising how time stood still during my enforced absence. Everything remains exactly as I left it. Clothes and shoes scattered carelessly across the room and floor, a half-filled glass of juice now welded to the wood laminate surface of my dressing table, my still-open study books pausing to await my return from lunch. Tears trickle down my cheeks, not for the nostalgia of returning to my material comforts but for the grief and loss of innocent expectation. The expectation that I could complete my schooling like any other teenager, that I could dress as I wish with the freedom to choose sleeveless shirts or low-cut dresses, to swim or sunbathe with the same lack of inhibition as my friends and peers, to worry about pimples or blackheads, not skin grafts or infections.

My life has changed and I need to learn to adapt and to embrace the changes; not with anger or bitterness or it will eat away at my spirit as sure as a malignant cancer, but with renewed hope and optimism that my life, although disrupted, will carry on, just differently than planned. T and I talk about the new and different life choices and opportunities that await *Me*. Once again I must choose the life that I must lead. I choose the path of the survivor not the victim. I choose to gain strength and courage by going forward with an unspoken faith and not to dwell fruitlessly on the vacuous question *why Me?* But to believe and accept with conviction that everything in the life I choose has a positive reason and outcome, even if I can't see or even begin to understand the why, how or what.

During the initial weeks following my discharge from hospital, I etch out new routines that alternate between being a domestic goddess, cooking, cleaning, sewing, reading, to that of a submissive slave chained to a strict regime of continuing pills and treatments. As much of my time is controlled by an enforced house arrest, incarcerated to minimise the risk of infection, I eagerly anticipate every variation to the increasing predictability of each day.

Regular visits from the district nurse who instructs *Me* how to bathe properly, clean and dress my wounds until sufficiently healed. The highlight of each month being denigrated to my outpatient visits to Mr. Plastics, the hospital consultant who continues to monitor and assess my skin grafts and who seems pleased that I have no post-operative complications *that might threaten the natural healing progression of my grafts*. After a few months of recuperation, I am bored. Really and truly bored. I am self-medicating and have mastered the discomfort of accommodating my second skin, my sexy off-white elasticised de-wrinkling vest that is now an undergarment for all my new self-styled and remodelled wardrobe.

I begin to envy Ray who habitually is the first to rise and cheerily goes off to his day centre every morning with an enthusiasm that shames *Me*. My vain preoccupation with appearance is in danger of disabling *Me* more than all the disabilities brushed aside by Ray every moment of every day. Ray loves his 'job'. I need a job. The realisation is so obvious yet it strikes *Me* like a bolt of divine insight. An even greater shock is securing a full-time job immediately following my first job application to be an operator with British Telecommunications, or BT as it is commonly known. My confidence and self-esteem soars as I realise that people simply see and accept *Me* as *Me*. The only person who seems to define *Me* by my accident is *Me*, although inevitably there are always some exceptions to any rule. They present with disarming impact in the personas of a young work colleague and the girlfriend and later wife of T's cousin, Kevin. Even in recollection my instinct remains that the first was uttered through innocent naivety and is forgivable, the latter rooted to petty vindictiveness and was deliberately crafted and timed for maximum humiliation.

Shortly after joining BT I found myself comfortable enough to drop my guard by disclosing some aspects of my accident and my subsequent emotions and feelings in confidence to a younger work colleague over a shared lunch. More thinking out loud than directing her response to *Me*, my young colleague, only two years younger than *Me* but closer to fourteen in maturity, speculates on how lucky I am to have a boyfriend who can accept my scarred appearance. This superficial conclusion to my shared inner feelings pierces my newly-found confidence as painfully as the boiling oil that scorched my flesh. No, I refuse to accept that self-pitying perspective. I am who I am as a person, not how others choose to perceive or define *Me* as a burns victim. With an air of reassured confidence, I raise my eyes to lock onto those of my young friend and state with genuine conviction *no you're wrong, T is lucky to have Me*.

My second brush with maintaining my self-esteem and dignity emulated from the girlfriend of T's cousin Kevin. Characteristically a malicious and manipulative person who could cut as effortlessly as an assassin's knife, she chooses to time her attempted humiliation in front of an audience of friends supporting *Me* to celebrate my first day of release from house arrest. Confident that I am safe from infection and well on the road to recovery, T organises an evening out with friends at our local pub. After an enjoyable evening, floating high on the company of friends expressing and sharing their genuine delight by welcoming *Me* back into their circle, with pure malice she chooses her moment to demolish my moment in the limelight. Just as I finish putting a fashion spin on my newly-acquired range of high-collared blouses and polo necks, she captures centre-stage by loudly declaring her confusion over my obsession with modesty. *After all, my friend who is a nurse tells me that every male who works in the hospital has had an eyeful of your crisped body.*

I feel the ground rupturing beneath my feet, preparing to swallow *Me* down to its darkest recess. Fighting back the tears I slowly regain strength from the gathering contempt that bonds my personal sense of humiliation to the collective but encouraging disdain on the faces of my wider circle of friends, male and female. Recognising that dignity and victory are won in allowing such a contemptuous lie to wither and die in its own vacuum, I turn my back as a gesture of dismissal and continue to feign a carefree assertion that polo necks will shortly become the must-have trendsetter for all teens and twenties.

At the time, my anger cemented a long legacy of contempt for unnecessarily nasty and vindictive people who attempt to elevate themselves through humiliating, embarrassing, belittling or dismissing others. Through reflection, rather than rekindling anger or contempt, I now experience a profound sense of pity and sadness. Pity that some people are so insecure, that to be noticed they need to resort to deflecting their own self-worthlessness onto others. Sadness, that rather than achieving the more elevated position sought, they simply feed their inherent insecurities and diminish the very attention and esteem that they so hungrily crave.

Shifting my recollected thoughts again, T throws my mind into conflicting chaos. Over Saturday morning coffee I notice and comment that he seems pensive and quiet. Looking serious and straight at *Me*, T declares *I've been thinking. I think that we should get married.* Slightly taken aback, not by the proposal, and I ask *is that seriously your marriage proposal?* but by the unexpected timing of being asked or more inappropriately told over coffee. My mind goes into overdrive, *how can I, Ray, Mum, Gran?* Reading my thoughts, T continues, *I love you. I have loved you from when we first spoke on the bus home from school. I want to spend my life loving you more and more.* Reading my hesitation, T gently reminds *Me* that my family will always remain my family. *We will both be there for them but also there for each other. You have your own life to live too. Live it. Live it with me by your side.*

I have my own life to live. Yes, I will live it.

Yes. Yes, I will, I accept. I would love to marry you. I love you too but you should have proposed properly to Me, down on one knee with a ring in your hand I rebuke. T smiles, *from now on we do all things together, and that includes choosing your ring.*

On the following Sunday T chooses his moment and 'informs' Mum, Ray and Gran of our decision. Ray and Gran grin at each other. Mum nods, before glaring at *Me* behind T's back with her disapproving face and continues with tidying the house as if T has just announced fish and chips for tea.

Determined to carry on and accepting that to win Mum over will be a war of attrition, but ultimately winnable, T and I go shopping for an engagement ring, settling to browse the selection available in a jewellery shop at the top of the main street in Lisburn, a busy provincial town eight miles west of Belfast. The lady is helpful and very accommodating as I try different rings from solitaires to cluster diamonds presented across several trays, each retrieved from behind the secure glass cabinets. We fail to be inspired. Thanking her and apologising that we are unable to choose, we turn to leave. *Stop. One of my rings is missing. Please give it back* she demands. Protesting our innocence to the obvious accusation of theft,

I suggest that it must have fallen onto the floor, *you look behind the counter and I'll look in front*. No ring is found. The lady's attitude hardens as she threatens to call the police. Raising my hands to gesture that we haven't taken her ring, the lady shouts *yes you have, it's there, on your sleeve*. Sure enough the ring is snagged on the underside sleeve of my mohair jumper. *It must have caught when I was lifting a ring from the tray*, I reasoned. *Yes, of course it did. Give it back and please leave my shop now*, she demands. T helps *Me* to extract the ring leaving a small pulled thread in its wake and we leave the shop without any further exchange of words. Outside, we look at each other more stunned than angry. Spontaneously we both laugh realising that the 'formalisation' of our engagement could so easily have been celebrated in a police cell. Had I seriously considered becoming a master jewel thief I think I would have gone better equipped than with just a mohair jumper to achieve my sleight of hand diamond heist.

Mum appears to rally a little more interest towards our forthcoming wedding, finally agreeing to accompany *Me* to Belfast to help choose my dress and to pick her mother of the bride outfit. Arriving just after midday in the city, we enter the renowned bridal shop, Jean Millar, located on Royal Avenue. Following a discussion with the sales advisor, I choose three distinctly different dresses to try. After an exhaustive effort to squeeze into the first, just managing to avoid stepping on the excessive train, I breeze from the changing room into the shop area to ask Mum what she thinks. *It's lovely, take it dear*. But it's not lovely, it's not the shape I want. *I'll try on one of the other dresses*.

If you must, is Mum's rhetorical response.

Maintaining an air of excitement, my second dress is an improvement on the first but still lacks a certain elegance I think.

Perfect, let's take it and let's go for lunch. You mean a liquid lunch I retort inwardly.

I'll just quickly try on this last dress, more out of mild curiosity to see what the most elegant, hand-laced, possibly one of the most expensive dresses on show would look and feel like. Fit for a princess to be married. Absolutely stunning, a dream for any bride to be. Stepping from the changing room I extend both arms in a flamboyant gesture of provocation. *Well?*

With hardly a glance, *beautiful, take it, now can we go?*
Alright, if you agree, I'll compromise on this one.

Removing the dress, I hand the dress to the sales assistant to box and wrap who takes it from *Me* managing to avoid all eye contact. By the time I return to the shop Mum has chosen her outfit, dress, hat, shoes, that, that and that all en route to the till and checkout.

We leave Jean Millar's at 1.30pm and go for lunch.

Despite the rockiest of roads, T and I meet at the altar on 13th March 1982 and exchange our vows to be declared, *husband and wife together.* Any forebodings that threatened to overshadow our special day evaporates as T and I enjoy an amazing and happy day with family and friends. Ray looks amazing and happy too in his role as groomsman. Doe and *Me* are reunited, with my big sister returning to Ireland to be by my side, and Mum is exceptionally well behaved and reminds *Me* of the Mum I knew and loved in Saul Street; elegant, generous, happy and loving.

Oh, how I have missed the Mum of my childhood.

Thank you Mum for making this the most special day for Me, simply everything that I could have wished for.

Acceptance and tolerance and forgiveness, those are life-altering lessons.

Jessica Lange

Chapter 8

A new family for *Me*

You don't choose your family. They are God's gift to you, as you are to them.

Desmond Tutu

T and I put the mortgage deposit down on our first house, a three-bedroom semi-detached in Tandragee just six miles from Portadown, almost a year before we married. Although familiar with our new home, having painted, decorated and part-furnished it in the months before marrying, this does not diminish my excitement for our new home after returning from a short honeymoon break in Dublin. The excitement for properly enjoying our new house, opening the many gifts and presents that will help to transform it into our first home together, compensating for shortening our honeymoon to just five days in anticipation of some crisis or other that would demand our immediate return.

Arriving home, T and I discover that Mum, in our absence, has indeed been having tantrums. Despite Doe's best efforts to keep things running smoothly, Mum has confiscated all our wedding gifts and presents and locked them in her garage. More a silly gesture of defiance at my decision to leave home, to abandon her, *your family, and for what, him*, T. Not a serious attempt to deprive us of our wedding gifts or an estrangement from *Me* or T, just a predictable welcome home from Mum and quickly resolved by the intervention of Uncle Robert before returning to England with Doe.

    A new life begins. Like most young couples we strive and struggle financially to build our nest. T works hard taking on a second job two evenings each week after work and on alternative Saturdays and Sundays. The pressures of sometimes feeling like passing ships helps to mask the facade of my increasing double life. With T, I'm happy and carefree, planning and building our futures together. Being loved for simply being *Me*, I thrive in T's arms that uphold *Me* with a peace and security beyond my past experience. A fragile and proxy peace that risks being shattered by the shrill ring tone of the telephone. A ring tone that sends shivers down my spine that inevitably summons *Me* back to the battle-weary frontline for yet another skirmish with Mum's bitter and twisted mind. Recriminations for finding my own life to live. Accusations for abandoning her, *for him*. Blame for all that is wrong and twisted and warped in the distorted reasoning mind of an alcoholic.

    Despite my longing to resist each call to action, to rebel against the inevitable summons, I know that I must respond if only to shield Ray from the next assault. I remain powerless to mother's beckoning call. The child in *Me* responds with the submission to drop everything and go. Fortunately, T's heavy work commitments provide opportunities to practise frequent infidelity within my new married life, pretending to be at home cleaning and cooking whilst scuttling across town and country to deliver gin. The bootlegger daughter quenching the thirst and soothing the anger that threatens to explode the more normal and respectable domesticity that I have created around *Me* with new friends and neighbours. I hate the duplicity, the lies, the total deceit. My conviction that it is easier to indulge the lesser of two evils, pits the fragility of my mind against the torment threatening my new life. I can't stop Mum drinking but I can preserve and protect my husband, my friends, my neighbours, from the embarrassing excesses that any enforced sobriety can induce with a volatile and unpredictable Mum.

Gradually my parallel lives merge and fuse so as to become inextricably linked.

To my new world I appear the dutiful daughter. I become intoxicated by this normal life that is only bought by the toxic duplicity that is my abnormal life. I need to conceive a way to reconcile the irreconcilable. The birth of our first child, Jonathan, or Jay, as T and I pet-name our beautiful baby boy, provides a temporary respite that breaks the cycle of Mum's self-destruction and my self-despair.

Without prompting, even Mum is captivated by her first grandchild. A new maternal instinct awakens in Mum as Jay accomplishes in an instant what I have failed to achieve in a lifetime. Sobriety. The Mum of my childhood returns. Happy, proud, generous and selfless.

My life feels transformed. Jay brings happiness, laughter and unconditional love into our lives. Doe flies home at every opportunity to be the doting aunt. Ray, the proud uncle regales Jay's every movement to the staff and friends at his day care centre and Mum metamorphoses into the caring grandmother. Jay brings renewed purpose into Mum's life, putting a sparkle back into her eyes as she focuses upon her *wee man*.

Gran enters her ninety-ninth year and we are all excitedly anticipating the special letter to come from Her Majesty Queen Elizabeth II that will mark her next centennial birthday. Regrettably Gran succumbs to illness and quietly passes away at home in the early spring of 1983, just eight months after Jay's birth and only falling short of her long-awaited Royal acknowledgement by a few short months. Gran's 'departure' at least witnessed an answer to her long-suffering prayers. The birth of a new generation paving the way for a peaceful departing release for the oldest generation; comforted by seeing a *miraculous healing* for the hurt and anger so often expressed by her own child for so long.

With T's support and encouragement, I take advantage of a voluntary redundancy opportunity to leave work to become a full-time mum for Jay. I feel I have at last discovered my true vocation in life. A life anchored around my son. Treasuring every moment of every day I can barely allow Jay to sleep with the excitement of motherhood. Barely out of nappies and just walking, I realise that I am unexpectedly expectant again. Despite occasional minor relapses, Mum proves herself as a trustworthy grandmother. Minding a two-year-old with another baby on the way, I begin to rely more and more upon my now stable Mum and begin to enjoy our new positive relationship together.

Saturday morning and Mum picks Jay and *Me* up to take us shopping for the expected new baby. T has gone to work early and doesn't expect to be home until late in the evening. The sun is shining and Jay is fed and sleeping contentedly in the baby seat as we drive the short distance to Rushmere Shopping Centre at Craigavon, on the outskirts of Portadown. I notice that Mum's driving is becoming more erratic. Initially distracted by Jay and my unborn kicking inside my tummy, I failed to notice the slurring in Mum's speech. Suddenly gripped by fear and panic I realise that Mum is drunk. Drunk, and driving *Me* with my children. Trying desperately to sound calm I ask Mum to stop the car. *Why?* she slurs more dismissively than questioningly.

Just stop the car now, I demand, louder and more strained than I intended. Mum glares back at *Me* with her menacing out of control eyes. *Watch the road*, I scream as the car crosses the white dividing line before careering back, tossing us recklessly in our seats. I scream, S*top now*. Whether it's the shock of my scream or the non-negotiable tone of my voice, but Mum suddenly veers across the road and the car ploughs to a stop with the nearside wheels firmly immobilised in a muddy roadside ditch. Shaking with rage, I storm from the car, remove Jay's buggy from the boot and secure my screaming toddler before venting my full anger at Mum. Snatching the car keys from the ignition I scream at Mum to *make your own damn way home* before stomping off with hot tears streaming down my face.

Relations with Mum become very strained again. As the months pass, despite my deep-rooted anger and frustration, I can't fail to recognise that Mum's drinking is beginning to take a more obvious and sinister toll upon her health. Protesting a small appetite, Mum only picks at her food and rarely finishes a complete meal. Increasingly, Mum rarely seems to eat anything of substance and has become noticeably thin and gaunt. Insisting that she speaks to a doctor, I arrange a home visit as a compromise for Mum refusing to visit the health centre. Showing obvious concern, the doctor immediately organises for Mum to be admitted into hospital for tests. Speaking privately with the doctor at the front door as he prepares to leave, the doctor expresses his grave concerns about the *impact that long-term alcohol abuse can have on a person's liver.*

Mum detests her time in hospital and implores *Me* to help her to *get out of this godforsaken place*. My emotions are in turmoil, as Mum needs proper care but is distraught with the thought of staying in hospital. I so want to help but I am distraught too at the thought that Mum is now beyond capable of looking after or caring for herself. I can't let Mum return home alone but neither can I go 'home' with her. I have my own child to care for and my own home to run. And, of course there's Ray to consider. Ray needs looking after too. What a mess. I want to bring them both to my house, to our home, with T and Jay, but that isn't fair on them. I just don't know which way to turn, how to do right without potentially wronging others. My mask slips and I confide my emotional turmoil to T.

Bring your Mum to our house. Ask your Uncle Jimmy to take Ray for a few days until your Mum has time to recover. You can't leave her to languish in hospital, she's not in a fit state to look after herself, much less Ray, and we have a spare room, so what's the problem? T asks with naive simplicity.

It's not that simple, she'll drive you nuts, I counter half-heartedly. *Your Mum only drives me nuts when I can't see what she is up to. If she moves in here at least we can both keep an eye on her. Besides, your Mum is too ill for mischief and you really don't have a choice. We're family. Your Mum comes to us and Ray goes to Jimmy. It's only complicated if you choose to make it so.*

T has good reason and right to not want Mum under his roof but knows too that my heart is breaking and his greater love for *Me* instinctively dismisses any sense of personal inconvenience or disruption. *She's my Mum now too so let's go bring her home.*

Ray goes to stay with Uncle Jimmy and Mum comes to stay with *Me*. Maybe not quite as simple as T made it sound but together we somehow arrive at our new domestic arrangement. Mum settles into the spare bedroom and I quickly adapt to my new role of home nurse. My baby is due in six weeks but it's a relief not to have to travel back and forth between Tandragee and Portadown.

Despite being disapprovingly allowed to discharge herself from hospital Mum remains very ill and her condition fails to respond to my constant care and attention. The doctor visits regularly and is preparing *Me* for the inevitability ahead.

After just two weeks, Mum's health deteriorates noticeably day by day. Ironically our intense time together creates an opportunity for renewed intimacy. Without words, the barriers of each pretending normality to the other melts away. An honesty, a greater openness to discuss past pains and hurts flows naturally without the usual confrontation, accusations or recriminations. Just a need to talk, to listen and to understand. To accept what we each say to each other without judgement or sentence. In the diminishing time frame, so much that seemed at the time so significant is intuitively dismissed or discarded, no longer worthy of repeated discussion. When time is short, even subconsciously short, if the underlying bond is rooted in love, a mother for her child and a child for her mother, a spirit of knowing prevails. What can't be expressed is simply felt and accepted. Repentance and forgiveness reciprocated one to each other without needing words or reason. To simply love and to be loved is sufficient reward.

As the end nears and with T's blessing, I take Mum into our marital bed and T respectfully and selflessly retreats to the spare room, allowing *Me* to be nearer still. To be there when the time comes. Sensing a need beyond what I can offer or give I ask Mum if she would like to speak and perhaps pray with T's Uncle Nick, an elder with the Elim Pentecostal Church. Mum nods, T makes the call and Nick comes quietly without fuss or fanfare.

Trying not to be intrusive and yet compelled to be near, as if called to bear witness for myself, I sit quietly on the top step at the end of the hallway to our bedroom, to listen and to wait. Nick gently engages with Mum first in conversation and finally in prayer, leading both Mum and indirectly *Me*, to a place of incomprehensible peace and quietness. Mum through words of comfort and assurance. *Me* through witnessing the burden of a troubled life lifted and an overshadowing emotional pain released. Two days later, in the early hours before the dawning of a new day, Mum slips quietly away. Holding Mum gently in my arms I gasp and sob at the realisation that my Mummy too has now 'departed'.

The memory of death evokes a new spiralling of thoughts and emotions, whipping up a whirlpool of lives sequentially marred and destroyed by alcohol dependency and abuse.

A perverse imagined game of spin the bottle jolts my memory coming to rest pointing accusingly towards Robin, the husband of my good friend Wilma. A man with such extraordinary talents and generosity imprisoned by his own memories of past experiences too strong to break the shackles of his addiction. A man driven to self-destruction that estranged him from family and friends to a life of isolation, loneliness and premature death. Why?

The bottle spins again pointing reprovingly towards Ian and Jade. Young neighbours introduced through our children's schooling who uncontrollably try to destroy each other's lives and their own. Lives abused causing their own children to witness a family's near-destruction as the alcohol blinds their path towards a sheer precipice. Jade institutionalised, a soul lost into a mental abyss. Ian surviving, to begin soberly picking up the shattered pieces of his life and those of his three dispersed and disorientated children. Why?

T's Uncle Nick and his wife Auntie Flo. Having emigrated to Spain after retirement to live out their remaining years close to their son and his family, both are killed instantly on a Sunday morning on their way to church by a young drunk driver recklessly careering home following a Saturday night binge-drinking episode. Why?

Uncle Jimmy, succumbing to a lifetime of whiskey 'nightcaps' that outwardly showed little or no impact, but inwardly triggers a progressive deterioration of his liver and kidneys. A man with incredible strength of character who immediately accepts self-responsibility for his daily indulgence and goes through 'cold turkey' to emerge from his unwitting dependency dry, healthier and fitter to enjoy a further ten years' extended life. Why?

And others. Extended family, friends, friends of friends. A cycle of dependent souls that drift in out of my life experience throughout the years following Mum's death. Why?

It is difficult to live without judging others. If you have to judge, then judge with love.

Debasiah Mridha

Chapter 9

Angel feathers surround *Me*

The golden moments in the stream of life rush past us and we see nothing but sand; the angels come to visit us, and we only know them when they are gone.

George Eliot

A pure white feather rests with unspoken assurance at my feet. I recognise its significance and an involuntary tear trickles down my cheek. As on many previous occasions my guardian angel shows her presence and, having captured my attention, whispers thoughts into my subconsciousness. Sometimes insightful, sometimes challenging or reproving, always thought-provoking. This morning, gently comforting. Mum is at peace. Recovering from her earthly wounds. Surrounded by those that love and care for her. Those who passed earlier. Helping her. Guiding her. Healing her. A better place, but never far. Always but a thought apart but never truly departed. I smile. I sense the warmth and love of Mum smiling back.

My spiritual beliefs have been woven into the fabric of my being over a long journey of self-discovery and reflection. From a childhood indoctrination into a Church of Ireland tradition and faith, inspired through regular service attendances at Down Cathedral, to the joy of singing in church and school choirs. Leaving Downpatrick for a nomadic wandering through differing dominations, never again feeling wholly settled or at one with a singular doctrine or divine absolute; choosing instead to seek and adopt my own composite of faiths. Christianity, traditional Anglican to Pentecostal, Hindu beliefs and testimonies of reincarnation, new age spirituality, tarot and future reading, Buddhist teaching of inner self. Times of confusion and dryness, other times of understanding and none. But always a recurring assurance and acceptance of the surrounding protection and watchfulness from my angels.

The more I strive to learn, to understand, to accept unconditionally, the more I feel confused, estranged, unable to fully embrace. And yet I find pathways to truths for personal belief and spiritual comfort from each of the many and varied faiths, beliefs and philosophies, each strengthened and emboldened by personal testimonies and stories of individual experiences retold. Of one universal God, many Gods, no God.

My memory isolates a moment in time knowing that Mum is dying, within a few short weeks separating the due date for our second baby. I'm in hospital for my final ultrasound scan and conscious that Mum may not be alive to see her new grandchild, so I ask the stenographer if she can tell *Me* the gender of my baby. She expresses a reluctance to give her opinion but I explain my reason for asking and apply just enough pressure for her to waver and then concede to my impassioned appeal.

At times of death and new life, the birth of my son, the impending death of my mum, the imminent arrival of my second child, so I discover a renewed thirst for truth. For meaning. For a purpose to living and dying. For *Me*.

Are you sure you want to know? Yes, I'm sure, I persist. Turning the screen monitor to give *Me* a better view, she traces the outline of baby with her finger and turns the question back on *Me. What sex do you think it is? A boy,* I reply. *I think so too but sometimes the scan isn't totally clear. If you can wait for another thirty minutes we have a newer, more accurate three-dimensional ultrasound scan machine. Much more accurate and clearer than this 2D scan.* I wait and the ward paediatrician conducts the new scan, somewhat excited to be showing *Me* her new toy. Again, the question of what sex is turned back on *Me, what sex do you see?* Distinctly a boy, *look you can see his gangly bits clearly. Yes, definitely a boy,* the paediatrician confirms.

Back home I can't wait to tell Mum in the hope that it might just give her something to focus upon. Something to give her the strength to fight the illness. To survive for. *Mum it's a boy, another grandson, a wee brother for Jay.* Looking at my bump, Mum smiles and with greater self-confidence than the paediatrician declares *if that's a boy I'm a fox!*

I smile, trust Mum to be contrary and know more than the paediatrician. My old Mum's back. Just maybe the new baby is all the incentive Mum needs to get better. I so wished, if only Mum was right. My life is surrounded with males; my husband, my son, my brother, even the cat is a tom. How I would so love a daughter.

Mum dies peacefully in my arms on 5th August 1986. Just sixteen days later and one week premature, I go into labour. T has gone off to work for starting at nine o'clock in the morning and, sensing something feels different, and exasperated by a restless night of dreams, disconnected thoughts, random words, not conversations, from and with Mum, I take a quick bath and almost immediately my contractions start. I telephone T while packing my hospital bag and patiently wait for T to return home. *I need to go to the dentist on the way to the hospital,* I disarm T as he arrives back home just before ten o'clock. Seeing his confused expression, I confidently predict that the baby *won't be here for a few hours yet,* vainly asserting that *I am not going into labour with a wobbly crown. I've telephoned the dentist and he is going to fix my crown on the way to the hospital.* Within the next hour my crown is firmly re-cemented and by lunchtime I'm in the final stage of giving birth.

You have a beautiful baby girl, the midwife declares, *congratulations Mum and Dad.*

Despite my discomfort, and probably a little more forceful than intended, I challenge the midwife. *No, you must be wrong, I'm having a boy. Yes, I know my dear, that's what your notes state but trust me, this baby is most definitely a beautiful baby girl. I guess the good Lord had his reasons for changing his mind,* she announces.

If it's a boy, I'm a fox. How did Mum know?

As T sits beside *Me* in the recovery ward, gently enfolding and protectively swaying *our beautiful daughter* in his arms, he grins and provocatively suggests *Johnny Cash had a hit song with 'A Boy Named Sue', perhaps we could write our version, a girl named Richard.*

Richard was the name we had chosen for our new son in the weeks before birth. I smile, *maybe not, I don't think the boy called Sue story ended well when he became a man.* Seizing the moment, I declare *her name is Andrea. Mum knew we were to have a girl, knew how much we wanted a girl, I feel she has interceded for us to have a girl.*

So why Andrea, why not just Anne? T prods. *I don't like the name Anne but I want Anne to be in the name, and the name An-drea came into my head the night before and has stayed with Me all day* I sheepishly explained, not really understanding my own line of reasoning.

Well if that's what you feel, Andrea it is then accepts T. And so, Andrea Rachel joins our little expanded family.

Poor T, returning to work the next morning, amidst all the excitement in the office someone asks *and have you agreed a name? Yes, it's,* and all T could think off was Richard. Try as he might, T embarrassingly could not recall the name I had 'chosen' for his new daughter, eventually declaring Andi to his confused and bemused colleagues. The irony of T accidentally abbreviating to a boy-sounding name was not lost on either of us and stuck as our family pet name for Andrea.

Late in the evening, after a succession of well-wishing visitors had left, family and friends all cooing and clucking around baby Andrea or Andi to her Dad, I checked again for the umpteenth time that my baby was comfortable and sleeping peacefully before shuffling off with some physical discomfort to find my own peace and solitude in the ward toilet cubicle.

Why do I feel that the toilet seat offers a place for quiet contemplation and refection? I smile and think of my Daddy's daily 'constitution'.

My mind is racing, full of jumbled emotions and disjointed thoughts. Grasping to make sense, to rationalise, to understand. Exhausted yet elated with joy and happiness. I recall a conversation with T's Uncle Nick, revealing my innermost desire for a baby girl and Nick counselling with his insightful wisdom *be careful what you wish for.* At the time, I was slightly dismayed at what I took to be a sinister warning, but now understood his words to have a fuller and more joyous meaning *be careful what you wish for… it just might come true.*

Despite my life appearing more complete, a husband who loves and adores *Me*, my beautiful three-year-old son, my precious gift of a baby daughter, the epitome of a 'gentleman's family', and yet my mind and imagination continue to collide. I fret about Ray, I love being reunited with Doe visiting but Doe is soon to return to her other life in Somerset. Thoughts of my long-departed father, my recently deceased mum. Thoughts of my newly-expanded family competing with my old disintegrating family. Threads of thought tightening here, unravelling there, loose, now redundant threads cut away. I see the tapestry of my life again from behind, unpicking the old picture, reworking anew, once again to create an emerging new tapestry that will inevitably begin to reveal the next stage of my continuing life journey.

Cutting through the random muddle of threads, my mind begins to focus upon a new, more physical intrusion. Staring intensely at the bathroom floor I begin to see, then recognise a shape, familiar and strangely reassuring. Soft and gentle in its quiet appearance, arriving with a distinctive understatement and yet signifying a commanding presence. Resting between my feet, barely visible beneath my ankle length Victorian-styled white cotton nightdress, rests a small white feather. As my eyes gain focus and recognition my mind dismisses the turmoil of the previous minutes and settles to listen for the accompanying message. Without audible words, I somehow discern, y*our Mum is with you and thanks you. Your gift will bring you the happiness and joy that I stole from you.* My eyes fill with tears and, as I sob uncontrollably, I can hear my own voice murmuring *thank you Mum, thank you.*

> *When we are touched by something it's as if we're being brushed by an angel's wings.*
>
> Rita Dove.

Chapter 10

The light comes to *Me*

The wound is the place where the Light enters you.

Rumi

Discharged from hospital, arrival home feels different for *Me*. Despite the emotional traumas from the previous weeks and months I feel strangely refreshed. No longer burdened by conflicting thoughts of past arguments or guilt, I begin to dwell only on the present. My time is filled with a crying baby, feeding times, dirty nappies, sleepless nights. Days spent juggling my baby's needs with those of her older brother, now vying for greater attention having discovered that little sis is too young for any abiding interest in his playtime interests or pursuits. I'm loving every minute of every day. My children become my whole world. A world free from grown-up worries or concerns. A world immersed in the innocence of childhoods. My job becomes one of nurturing and loving, of being loved back unconditionally. For six months, life for *Me* has transcended into heaven on earth. Each day I awake with a sense of excitement and anticipation for the day ahead. A time for healing and recovery, of building strength and acquiring new coping tools for the new tasks ahead.

T feels drawn back spiritually to his earlier childhood roots and is attending Elim Pentecostal Church regularly. I share in his joy and happiness and accompany T to many Sunday services rejoicing in the uplifting songs of praise and celebration. I recognise a peace and contentment in those around us and strive to capture this sense of fulfilment but somehow, although I feel empathy for their apparent happiness and contentment, I cannot discover or capture for *Me* an unconditional or blind acceptance for their black and white beliefs. A shared emotional uplifting but a slight jealousy that, try as I do, I somehow cannot take the final required step of unquestioning faith that others seemingly find easier to embrace.

While T pursues a greater understanding through the pages of his Bible, for *Me*, I feel drawn more and more towards the literature of spiritualists and mediums. Testimonies of past lives and insights into the afterlife. Journeys beyond as told by returning souls and those whose lives are transformed. Stories and explanations of angels and guardian angels, chakras and self-healing. 'Saved' lives and lives reincarnated. My appetite for searching out new authors, exploring and testing differing pathways to enlightenment, is unquenchable.

Discovering a spiritual perspective in a simple book, *Embraced by the Light* by an American author Betty Eadie, unleashes an avalanche of comparable authors. From the spiritual guidance and teachings of Doreen Virtue to the sometimes differing 'worlds' of mediumship advocated by Doris Stokes, Mia Dolan, Rita Rogers, Betty Shine and many other acclaimed mediums. A myriad of testimonial afterlife journeys as retold by Jacky Newcomb and Theresa Cheung point *Me* towards healing angel stories by Francesca Brown and Helen Parry Jones and onward into therapeutic, regression and progression techniques as proffered by Dr Brian Weiss. The list goes on and on. Each captivating within their own respective writings, each giving spiritual clues, advice, guidance, direction or teaching. Sometimes complementing each other's perspective, sometimes contradicting. My journey seems endless and confusing.

Gradually I begin to realise that perhaps kernels of truth and enlightenment exist in each and all, but from the perspective of each author's own personal journey and experience. Each submission shaped and influenced by their own respective life experiences, personal interpretations manifesting into beliefs that become advocated faiths represented to others as the exclusive spiritual map to follow. But if each map is written to assist the personal journey for every individual to follow for their own life journey, can their personal or unique map fully or truthfully assist *Me* in my life journey? Should I not learn to draw my own map for my own personal journey? Certainly, listen and learn from those who journey before *Me*, but perhaps my personal journey is destined to take *Me* to a different end. My life's end. My life's purpose. Not the end as designated by any one or more renowned or celebrated authors, but as written by *Me*, as my own author, for my own life journey. Just as I have already discovered and accepted that the life I lead is the life that I choose, I begin to accept the insightfulness of others but with a much more open and challenging mind; as much as I apply a healthy cynicism towards relying too exclusively upon the 'trip advisor experiences' of another who may have travelled a similar journey before *Me*.

I have long learned that not all journeys lead to identical places or locations or share an identical or even common experience. Sometimes the same path can solicit a completely different appreciation and outcome, even if we stringently follow the same route map to the same destination. So too is my experience and journey through traditional and evangelical Christianity. I share T's excitement for the journey he is travelling but my harbouring passion towards my angels and the inherent animosity actively voiced by many within the wider Christian faith, censors my freedom to fully voice or express my underlying faith and belief in the angels that I believe surround, protect and guide *Me*. I struggle with understanding this abject rejection and antagonism towards angels when the Authorised King James Version of the Bible references angels 109 times throughout the Old Testament and an even greater 180 times within New Testament books.

Although I have always felt protected, even as a child I readily adopted the concept of angels watching over *Me*, but my curiosity to actively explore this tabooed dimension is only truly ignited shortly after T marries *Me*. A friend suggests visiting a woman in Poleglass, a social housing estate on the outskirts of Lisburn sprawling towards Belfast. Despite my misgivings I am persuaded to *go for a giggle*. My friend telephones to make an appointment and three weeks later we set off, more in anticipation for an evening's entertainment than for any serious pursuit into the world of future telling. As a distraction from my tendency to giggle when nervous or anxious, I take along a notebook and pen to help capture the salient insights into what the future might hold for *Me*; in truth, to enable *Me* to distract from my nervousness by allowing *Me* to ignore the common courtesy of maintaining eye contact while still listening to the medium. To not cause offence by giggling as I feign total concentration upon recording her foretellings to help with my future recollection for all that is said. Entering her home, I am immediately taken back by the warm and sincere welcome into her home adorned with angels, pictures and figurines that dominate the ambience from the entrance hall through into every room. Exuding a calm quiet confidence, she begins to talk, and continues talking, without prompting or probing *Me* to subtlety gain any insightful direction from *Me*. The flow of words washes over

Me while I frantically try to capture the essence of everything she is telling *Me* until finally, after almost forty minutes, she ends as she began, reclining back into her chair and reverting once again to the trivia of small talk to indicate our time of clairvoyance together has come to an end.

Back home, T mischievously interrogates *Me* with a healthy cynicism that masks his true curiosity. Despite my forty-minute 'consultation' my copious notes reveal only three references of any significance worth recalling. The woman foretold seeing *Me* surrounded by feathers, that our son would travel extensively and that our daughter would be born under a veil of death. At this time, I have no idea of the significance of feathers in my life; having just got married, we have no children nor any idea if we are to be blessed with future children, and I have absolutely no idea what she meant by being born under a veil of death. Following a little bit of smug ribbing from T, I consign my notes and experience of future-telling down to an interesting but mostly entertaining evening.

The following years allow *Me* to now view this earlier encounter through the reflective lens of time and with the benefit of my life more lived. Some years after this now long-forgotten consultation, I open my front door to be mesmerised by a semi-circular arrangement of pure white feathers, spanning the door from frame to frame. The plumage so perfectly arranged that I could not fail but be struck by its resemblance to a miniature rampart guarding the entrance to our home, surrounding *Me* with an army of ministering and protecting angels. A prelude to the recurrence of a single white feather that appears to *Me* with regular frequency and to T as an occasional visitor to say hello on many unrelated occasions and at varying locations throughout our lives together.

Andi was, as I now understand, born under the veil or shadow of Mum's death.

Jay, always a homebird, suddenly announces at twenty-one years of age after graduating from university that he intends to travel to New Zealand and possibly onward to Australia. A solo trip for at least twelve months, reasoned and designed to expand his practical experience for developing a career as a physiotherapist specialising in the treatment of sports-related injuries. A career progression beyond what the local Health Trusts can offer, excepting that to self-organise this migration to the opposite side of the globe without a safety net of friends or relatives to greet him upon arrival, seems to *Me* uncharacteristically either very courageous or extremely foolhardy. Either way, Jay fulfils his ambition and opens a Pandora's box for global travelling that subsequently witnessed him exploring extensively across Europe, South East Asia and North America over the following decade.

The woman's future-telling has come to pass, albeit over a span of time not obvious when first foretold.

The intervening and subsequent years of my life lived have consolidated my faith and belief towards accepting an assortment of what, for *Me*, I can only interpret as spiritual interventions, guidances and unexplainable occurrences and synchronicities. Random thoughts of past and present friends and acquaintances entering my head to be followed shortly by a face-to-face encounter or telephone call from that same person. A course of action contrary to my plans entering and dominating my thoughts until I capitulate and change my planned direction, to subsequently realise that my initial planned course or action would have led to danger, heartache or distress for *Me* or others around *Me*. A heightened sensitivity that enables *Me* to discern an unspoken hurt, distress or need in others, friends and strangers alike, with a confidence to draw alongside to offer a supporting intercession without intrusion that may cause further distress.

This natural ability or gift, as others have described this part of my personality, has introduced *Me* into a more accepting and ever-widening circle of friends, representing a peculiarly diverse and seemingly incompatible collective of ages, backgrounds, personalities, interests, faiths, beliefs and none.

The longer I live, the more I come to rely upon listening to the unspoken murmurings that stir my thoughts and heart to guide my words and actions. My guardian angel? Perhaps. I trust in the discernment, even if I have never been properly introduced to the named personality of a guardian angel for *Me*.

> *For you have delivered me from death and my feet from stumbling, that I may walk before God in the light of life.*
>
> Psalm 56:13

Chapter 11

The carer in *Me*

I sought my soul, but my soul I could not see. I sought my God, but my God eluded me. I sought my brother and I found all three.

Unknown

Six months into my heaven on earth sabbatical, enjoying exclusive time with my children, and life unexpectedly imposes another unanticipated twist. Following Mum's premature departure, Uncle Jimmy offered to take Ray into his home, a small detached bungalow bought for him by Mum shortly after we relocated to Portadown. Uncle Jim, being a confirmed bachelor, lacked many of the domestic skills necessary for maintaining a home but, with my hands full cradling a new baby and juggling the active needs of a toddler, he presents the most trusted person to become Ray's surrogate father of necessity. I organise for the sister of a close friend of mine, Beth, to provide a weekly house-cleaning service for the boys and take personal responsibility for the weekly wash, embarrassed that anyone beyond *Me* might be asked to wash their 'smalls'. Uncle Jimmy can cook, basic food, but at the very least a hot daily meal, and despite his domestic shortcomings he cares dearly for Ray, sharing in his passion for old time slapstick comedy.

Many a weekly visit finds the boys laughing and giggling together uncontrollably over repeat broadcasts of David Jason and Nicholas Lyndhurst wheeling and dealing in *Only Fools and Horses*, Reg Varney, Bob Grant and Stephen Lewis misbehaving *On the Buses* or Barbara Windsor, Sid James and Kenneth Williams frolicking about in any one of a dozen or more *Carry On* films; many names becoming household friends, popping in to entertain us regally over the coming years. Headlining Ray's list of favourite television shows is *Coronation Street*, which over the many years of avid viewing is to become Ray's 'mastermind' specialist subject at any pub quiz.

Everything is gently moulding into a settled routine. Uncle Jimmy helps Ray to shave, wash and dress, not necessarily coordinated with matching colours, but at least clothed and warm. After preparing Ray his breakfast, Uncle Jimmy waits until Ray is collected by the 'big white bus' each morning and safely en route to his day care centre, and only then does Uncle Jimmy set off to his own work as a delivery driver for a local cash and carry wholesaler; a job that takes Uncle Jimmy throughout the six counties, and builds a driving knowledge that enables him to take Ray on Saturday afternoon excursions to many of his delivery towns and villages, most often to his favourite county Tyrone. Most Saturday mornings, whilst T is working, I bundle the children into the car for our weekly adventure to Uncle Jimmy's house. Quality time for Jimmy and Ray to play with the children while I clean and tidy the house before Beth arrives on the Monday to clean and tidy the house. Sundays are reserved for family lunch together at our home in Tandragee with roast beef or chicken and all the trimmings followed without exception by Ray's favourite dish, dessert, any dessert.

Life for *Me* is bobbling along with a gloriously monotonous predictability. Mother and Toddlers' group each morning, shopping in the early afternoon, preparing evening dinner for T before he dashes off to his second job on alternate evenings.

On the evenings that T is not double-jobbing, it's off to visit Uncle Jimmy and Ray for an hour or two before returning to prepare the children for bed, then settling down to catch up on a little television for myself with T.

Friday evening, snuggling up to T on the family room settee and listening to the familiar opening tune of *Coronation Street*, my thoughts drift towards Ray, knowing that he too will be settling down to watch his favourite programme. The contentment of this assurance is suddenly interrupted by the loud shrill from the telephone situated on the hall table below the stairs. Fearing the noise will waken the children, I bound into the hall, snatching the handset on the second ring tone. *Beth hello, what a surprise, how are you?* My mind re-editing my words, a surprise yes, Beth never telephones *Me*, how are you, translating into how is Ray, is everything OK? *I'm sorry to call, it's your Uncle Jimmy, I don't know why, but I was passing his house and I just felt the need to check in on them. Jim's not at all well. He looks absolutely dreadful, can you come into town?*

I'm on my way Beth, give Me fifteen minutes.

Leaving T to mind the children, I arrive to find Uncle Jimmy tightly wrapped under a blanket, pale and sweating, slumped in his armchair. Barely coherent, he tries to dismiss his condition as just *a touch of flu*. Turning to Ray, who suddenly looks terrifyingly guilty that he has done something wrong, I ask *how long has Jimmy been like this? From yesterday. I didn't go to 'work' today, I stayed off to mind him.* Looking at the uneaten bowl of now soggy cornflakes sitting at the side of Uncle Jimmy's chair, my heart explodes with concern for Jimmy and love for Ray for his valiant efforts to be grown up and responsible. Recognising that Uncle Jimmy is in no fit state to look after Ray and Ray, despite his best intentions, is not capable of properly caring for Jimmy, much less himself, I take control. *Right, let's pack a few clothes, you are both coming home with Me until this 'flu' passes.* Uncle Jimmy tries to protest, *but the children?*

It's *time then that they built up their immunisation* and with that, the move is on.

Two hours later we arrive home, announcing to T that we have two house guests. With typical unquestioning patience and understanding, T immediately begins to reorganise our modest three-bedroom semi-detached to now accommodate four adults and two children. Andi's cot is relocated into our bedroom allowing Uncle Jim to sleep in the single bed prepared for the day when the cot is no longer required. Jay is transferred from his single bed in the adjacent bedroom into our double bed for the night until we can source a smaller camp bed that can fit parallel to his bed, now commandeered for Ray. Everyone is fast asleep again before midnight, except T and *Me*. Feeling exhausted, T looks at *Me*, gently kisses *Me* on the lips and assures *Me*, *we'll cope*.

Too ill to leave his bed, I telephone the surgery and arrange for the on-call doctor to make a house visit. Having built a relationship with the district doctor during Mum's last days at our home, the doctor arrives late morning and immediately goes to check on Uncle Jimmy, closing the bedroom door to consult privately. After what seems an age, the doctor comes down the stairs and asks to speak with *Me* in the family room. *Your Uncle is very ill. No, it's not flu, although the symptoms could be mistaken. I suspect that Jim may have damaged his liver, through excessive drinking.* Genuinely confused I question his diagnosis, *but Jim doesn't drink, not like Mum, I've never seen him touch a drop.* The tear trickling down the side of my cheek seems to trigger a compassionate response from the doctor whose own eyes glaze with an empathy of 'knowing'. *Not like your Mum* but Jim was honest and admitted that he has *taken a glass of whiskey every evening for over twenty-five years to help him sleep. Modest drinking, but the cumulative effect over so many years has caused complications. Trust me, Jim didn't realise the significance of his daily 'nightcap'; the damage is in a very early stage and, if he stops drinking anything with alcohol, he stands a good chance of making a reasonable recovery. If he doesn't stop, well, you know the consequences.*

He'll stop, he's stronger than Mum, he'll stop for Me and for Ray.

If he can stop, it won't be easy on him, or you. I'll give you a prescription to mitigate against the side effects of withdrawal. Make sure he drinks plenty of fluids.

After the doctor bids his farewell, sitting by the side of his bed, I hold Jim's hand and we talk, and talk some more. *You'd better go to my coat pocket.* Removing a quarter bottle of Jameson's Irish Whiskey, *let's start by emptying that down the sink,* Jimmy declares.

Sometimes naivety and ignorance are the best tools to get the job done, particularly when not knowing what sudden withdrawal can do. Mum may have curtailed her drinking on occasions but, on reflection, never demonstrated any of the consequences endured by Uncle Jimmy experiencing 'cold turkey'. What a horrible American expression that in no way fully elucidates the experience of sudden alcohol withdrawal. With hindsight and with the greater maturity that I have now, perhaps the kinder path would have been through gradual withdrawal. But, just as Uncle Jimmy decided one day to stop smoking and never again lit a cigarette, so too, he approached his withdrawal from alcohol dependency with the same resolve and determination. Initially the first week was tolerable for Jimmy and manageable for *Me*. Irritability I anticipated, having experienced plenty with Mum. Feeling tired and unsteady when he got out of bed to go to the toilet across the first floor landing was to be expected, as his appetite barely exceeded a half-bowl of soup daily. During the second week, Jimmy's lack of concentration gives way to confusion, extreme difficulty sleeping and hallucinations.

Around three o'clock one morning, T and I are suddenly woken by shouts and screams from the bedroom hallway. Jumping from bed we find Jimmy desperately attempting to climb into the hot-press cupboard. *What are you doing Jim? I've got to escape through this window. The soldiers, they're coming to kill me. I need to get out.*

Week three is the worst. Jimmy's whole body is trembling. Sweating profusely, I can't dismiss his pounding headaches. I can't give him any more paracetamol tablets or I'll be personally responsible for killing him. Jimmy's constant feeling of nausea and vomiting makes taking food almost impossible. I'm pumping liquids into Jimmy to avoid dehydration but his stomach is so engorged I'm horrified to enter his room, our newly-painted nursery, only to see orange-coloured fluid sprayed across the walls and ceilings. I'm convinced that the internal pressure building within Jimmy has excreted itself forcefully through his stomach lining.

Week four brings relief. Most symptoms have eased. Despite feeling shaky and suffering infrequent palpitations, Jimmy is beginning to recover. Soup graduates to small meals. His concentration is returning and he begins to talk about going back home. *Let's see how you feel at the end of the week, show Me that you can finish your dinner.* With characteristic determination Uncle Jim is back on his feet by the end of the week.

We need to go back home, Jimmy declares. I negotiate a compromise, *I will take you back home, but Ray stays with Me, just for a while longer. You need more time to recover, let Me care for Ray until you are feeling much better.*

Uncle Jimmy returns to his own house on Saturday, four weeks from the day he arrived, and Ray remains with *Me*, permanently.

> *Whether I or anyone else accepted the concept of alcoholism as a disease didn't matter; what mattered was that when treated as a disease, those who suffered from it were most likely to recover.*
>
> Craig Ferguson

Chapter 12

Teaching *Me*

Life is a succession of lessons which must be lived to be understood.

Helen Keller

Ray is back home with *Me*, where he has always belonged, and yet it takes two house moves and twice as many years before he finally utters the words *our home* during a conversation with T. Up until this time always referring to his new home as *T's and your house.*

As memories of Ray gather like clouds in my mind, a fresh storm of emotions, unprecedented in strength and clarity rain down and through *Me*. My heart rate pulsates until I feel breathless, drenched with such love that I am unable to comprehend our pending separation once more. I recall my childhood promise to be a *constant companion* for Ray. A promise failed so often but one that becomes the reality of our lives reunited for the past thirty years.

Initially I did not recognise the emotional or psychological damage sustained by Ray through his years of insecurity surviving with Mum. Sustained verbal abuse, hurting and scarring deeper than sticks and stones. A stranger to *Me* in our own home. A timid but clumsy teddy bear comes to mind. Each time I gaze towards Ray, looking into his doleful chestnut brown eyes, my maternal instinct flares and I simply want to wrap my arms around my big teddy bear to comfort and protect him from ever experiencing hurt and betrayal again. Ray strives to be unobtrusive, compensating for his inability to help around the house by attempting to live independently within the family routine. Rising early to wash and dress, making sure that he is clear from the bathroom before the morning household rush hour begins. Cooking his own breakfast, toast and a boiled egg, an attempt at shaving with his battery-operated shaver. Simple basic living skills practised at his day centre, but the personal grooming somehow always falling short of an acceptable standard and requiring some sensitive adjustments before his big white bus arrives. On busy mornings, the battery shaver must suffice, but gradually T introduces Ray to wet shaving to help remove the perpetual dark shadows across his cheeks and chin that elude the battery shaver. As T often jokes *I'm the only man who needs to shave twice daily before breakfast.* However, introducing Ray to wet shaving nearly ends in disaster when holidaying with Doe. Without T's steadying hand, Ray finds shaving foam and a razor in the bathroom and proceeds to shave himself before Doe discovers him slashed and bloody across most of his face. Thankfully superficial, but shaving joins Ray's ever-growing list of *thank you but no, I tried that once and I didn't like it.*

Gradually, ownership for dressing and more latterly for personal hygiene is shared by T and *Me*. We adopt the principle that Ray is an equal within our home. His obvious physical disabilities and restricted mental abilities are simple challenges to be overcome rather than barriers to progress. Rather than cushioning Ray from everyday risks and dangers, my philosophy to Ray becomes *manage the risks and if you break your legs, well, we'll simply fix them again.* For the most part, this 'can do' rather than 'can't do' attitude seems to work. Slowly

Ray rebuilds his own self-confidence, leading to greater self-belief and a noticeable improvement in his self-esteem. I call it Ray's *self-help programme*. Despite the potential for any number of slips, trips and falls, particularly during moving home three times, Ray only sustained physical injuries when our guardianship was delegated to his day care team.

With Jay settled in primary school and Andi safely in the charge of a home child minder, I reluctantly return to work, but delighted that T's double-jobbing enabled *Me* to enjoy five wonderful years at home with my children and the space to devote special catch-up time with Ray. A few years later, coming home more excited than had Andi been offered her own little pony, Ray announces that he is going horse riding. After some gentle probing, it transpires that his Centre has organised an introductory lesson at a facility endorsed by Riding for the Disabled, this coming Saturday morning. Ray on a horse, the thought terrifies *Me*. Well, you do tell him *to reach for the stars and this puts him six feet closer* quips T, not very helpfully. *OK*, I concede reluctantly, *but we're all going on Saturday to make sure Ray's safe. Maybe they'll have a small donkey for him to try first.*

Saturday is a success, watching Ray proud as punch being led around the soft enclosure brings a tear to my eye. My brother horse riding, Mum would be turning in her grave. Afterwards, the instructor leads Ray on his horse across the paddock to talk with T and *Me*. My protective instinct points out that the helmet Ray is wearing looks like an *undersized English 'bobby's' hat perched on the top of his oversized head.*

Ah, today was just a trial to see if Ray could manage to mount a horse. By next Saturday he will have his own properly-sized riding hat.

And will he always be led around this soft enclosure? fearful of the height that Ray would fall from if he lost his balance.

We don't ever go on the road and Ray will always have a volunteer guide walking alongside holding the reins to control the horse, he assures *Me*.

Earning my trust, I agree that Ray can start the following Wednesday on a six-week programme and can't help but smile looking up into Ray's beaming face. He knows how to twist *Me* around his little finger to get what he wants without barely asking. Looking at T, I nod towards Ray, *John Wayne junior.* T shakes his head and smiles.

Over the next four weeks Ray arrives home chirping like a canary, my horse this, my horse that. What next I'm thinking, sack the bus driver and buy him a horse to commute to 'work'. The following Wednesday I have just returned to my station after lunch as a BT telephone operator, when the supervisor comes to my desk and tells *Me* that I have a personal call, *you can take it in the manager's office.* My heart is exploding, you aren't allowed personal calls, something bad has happened. The short distance to the manager's office overlooking the open-plan telephonist stations feels like the 'green mile'. Something's happened to T, to Jay at school, the childminder has dropped Andi, Uncle Jimmy's had a relapse... *hello?*

Hello, this is Ray's Centre, I'm afraid Ray's had an accident, a fall from a horse. He's been taken to A&E at Craigavon Area Hospital by ambulance. Can you meet him there? I can't recall if I even replied, I dropped the telephone handset and looked at my supervisor discreetly hovering in the doorway with shock and terror suddenly etched across my face. *Go, take your coat and go,* she says.

Arriving at A&E I race blindly past the registration desk and straight through the treatment room curtains. Fortunately, Ray is in the first cubicle lying on his back on a treatment bed. Ray turns his head to reveal a scratched face and a sheepish grin. *I fell. It wasn't the horse's fault, I just fell.* I cry and Ray cries, not because he's in pain, simply because if I cry he knows something must be wrong or bad and he cries too. *As Ray bumped the back of his head on the tarmacked road, he needs an X-ray and we'll be transferring him to a ward for observations overnight as a precaution,* explains the treatment nurse.

Not for the last time I insist on staying the night and organise a blanket to try and catch a few hours' sleep in the visitors' armchair beside Ray's bed.

Waking with discomfort at three in the morning I look up and Ray is staring wide-eyed straight at *Me. I feel bad. You don't have a proper bed to sleep in.* How typical, Ray bangs his head, maybe cracks his skull and his only concern is for *Me.*

A time later I discover that the Riding Centre never got around to ordering a helmet to fit, took Ray for a trot out onto adjacent country roads and the volunteer guide was walking beside her friend who is leading the horse in front of Ray's horse. Sometimes there are good reasons why people cannot always offer unconditional trust towards others, even those with the best intentions.

A few years later my trust is abused once more. Again, I take a personal telephone call in work. *Ray's been knocked down by a bus. He's been taken to A&E by ambulance. Can you go to him?* Within twenty minutes I'm standing again by Ray's treatment bed. *A broken collarbone* explains the nurse. *He's very lucky, it could have been much worse.* How much worse can it get for someone with limited mobility and dependent upon a walking aid to also now manage with restricted use of his arm and upper body for weeks?

Following a protracted investigation, it transpires, but only after strong persistence and the threat of legal action, that Ray was visiting a Community Centre to take part in Boccia, a form of chair bowls popular within disability sports. Having assisted Ray from the bus, he was left to cover the distance from the bus to the Centre entrance on his walking aid, unsupervised. The driver, 'distracted', begins to reverse the bus into a parking position in front of the entrance knocking Ray to the road, causing him to fracture his collarbone. A lot worse had the driver not reacted to someone screaming, just managing to stop the rear bus wheel inches from Ray's head. On this occasion, I wavered my instinct to understand that accidents can happen and to forgive in favour of pursuing the truth. A truth that might ensure that proper lessons are learned and not simply brushed aside, in the hope that any new procedures introduced might avoid similar incidents inflicting injury or death to Ray, his friends or any other vulnerable person.

Managing to wash, dress and feed Ray become priority caring routines for T and *Me* in the weeks following his accident. Although the fracture heals, a little bit more of Ray's independence is stripped, never to fully recover. Ray returns to self-dressing, seeking approval from *Me* each morning that he has chosen something appropriate to wear. This morning Ray calls *Me* to our daily inspection but I ask T to give his approval. T slumbers out of bed and staggers bleary-eyed into the top hall for *Me* to be woken for a second time by T's hysterical laughing. I bounce out of bed to see Ray holding onto the rail at the top of the stairs wearing ten-year-old Andi's three-quarter-length Lycra joggers. A sight not decent to fully describe and impossible to imagine how Ray even managed to fully squeeze his twelve-stone frame inside so tiny a pair of joggers.

It's summer and time for Ray to visit his 'second favourite sister' as I jokingly describe Doe. An annual pilgrimage to Somerset for Ray to hold court with dear friends from Doe's village, summoned to visit the king with sweets, cakes and the perennial Daniel O'Donnell CD or video. In the earlier years, I travel with Ray on his flights to and from Bristol Airport but, as our confidences grow, I begin to trust Ray to travel on his own, supported by pre-organised airline assistance and with Doe waiting at arrivals. Always tears at departure and tears upon arrival, outbound and inbound. And yet, the tales tell a different story of fun with the airline stewardesses, chat and banter with his travelling companions seated left and right, and Coca-Cola. A constant supply of cola throughout the flight that always creates a crisis call of nature immediately upon entering each airport arrivals area. This annual reunion with Doe offers respite for T and *Me* and a time to focus fully upon our growing children.

Our most ambitious trip is organised for Florida, an end of primary school reward for Jay with flights to Orlando departing from Dublin Airport rather than the much closer Belfast International Airport. A corresponding flight is organised for Ray to also depart from Dublin to Bristol to coincide taking off a few hours before us and scheduled to return via Belfast International Airport a few days following our return from Disney World. All's fine until we present Ray at check-in only to realise that T has confused the check-in and departure times and the ticket desk is in the process of closing. After a frantic negotiation, the embattled check-in assistant reluctantly prints Ray's boarding pass for T, points in the direction of his departure gate but warns T that the flight is presently boarding and that unless they arrive in the next five minutes *the flight will depart without Ray*. To depart without Ray means to cancel our flights to Disney. With no time to check Ray's bag through the baggage carousel, T needs to carry Ray's bag and push Ray's wheelchair to the departure gate in time to make the flight. T sets off immediately with hardly time for a goodbye. After about ten yards, T sees a sign indicating the gate direction with a helpful '15 minutes walking distance' warning. Placing the case on Ray's lap, T instructs Ray to hold tight and sets off galloping at speed through the busy terminal. T instructs Ray to *shout Ray, move, move*. Ray obeys immediately and the corridor parts like the Red Sea allowing T to navigate a speedway track straight through to the departure gate, much to the disgust and *tut, tut, disgraceful* disapproving remarks following from sidestepping passengers. Although all the other passengers are boarded, the crew allows Ray to board with hardly a word from T, who needs at least ten more minutes to recover his breath. At Bristol Airport Doe meets Ray but can't understand why he took no Coke on the flight and, for the first visit ever, did not have a toilet crisis upon arrival. Apparently, according to the wheelchair porter assisting Ray to arrivals, Ray hasn't uttered a word from getting onto the aeroplane at Dublin. Poor Ray, just one of his many unusual experiences sharing his life with *Me*.

As with most school children, our children too occasionally arrive home from school with a note warning of an outbreak of head lice, or 'nits' as they are more commonly known, and advising parents to take appropriate action. Battle stations. The lotion is bought from the local pharmacy and administered immediately. To Jay, to Andi, to Ray, to T and finally to *Me*. The whole family is forced to sit patiently whilst the lotion does its job. Next the beds are stripped and every piece of bedding washed and tumble dried in case one or more 'nits' escape and are lurking to re-infest. While the bedding is being washed, next out comes the 'nit' comb, always a great amusement to Ray who teases the children until it's his turn to sit in complete indignation while I go big game hunting across his head. An exercise endured by all on a few occasions during primary schooling without capturing a single prisoner.

Worse is still to come for Ray as I overreact to a skin rash, convincing myself that he has contracted scabies. I find the strongest skin treatment available over the counter and strip Ray naked to paint the thick white cream all over. After a short time, Ray calls to T for help, pointing embarrassingly to his privates, waving his hand frantically to cool the cream's reaction to his more sensitive parts. T looks pained and sympathetic before breaking into song with the Jerry Lee Lewis classic 'Great Balls of Fire'.

Over the years I begin to recognise previously undiagnosed traits of autism in Ray's behaviour and personality. Happy to wear pyjamas in bed but only if allowed to keep his underpants on all night, only allowing his underpants to be changed in the morning. Ray cannot go to sleep without wearing his socks and will not wear an outdoor coat unless it has a hood, even if it's not raining. Although Ray eats most of anything placed in front of him, if given a choice he will only ever ask for chicken and chips, a problem exacerbated by allowing Ray the dignity to order his own lunches at his day centre necessitating a repetitive game of *eat your vegetables* at home. Not a problem when it comes to sweets. Although in the earlier years Ray gravitated towards sweets that T didn't enjoy, as their friendship grows Ray now selflessly chooses sweets that T favours, even if T's sweet of choice is Ray's least favourite. Ray's choice of films and music verges on Obsessive Compulsive Disorder (OCD). Despite a wide choice of DVDs to watch or CDs to enjoy, Ray always tends to replay the same selected disc over and over until either T or one of the children, out of tortured frustration, threatens to destroy the recording, more often hiding the DVD or CD, forcing Ray to choose a new title.

Meeting television or recording stars provides some of the greatest moments for Ray. Over the years, personally meeting a 'celebrity' on one or more occasions makes each a 'friend' for life. Someone to name-drop with total irrelevance or disconnect to the direction of any conversation. Not to impress, but simply to ensure that everyone can gain pleasure too from asking about how he met each one and what they talked about. Top of Ray's *I met* list is the Irish singer Daniel O'Donnell, closely followed by the broadcasters Gloria Hunniford and Gerry Kelly, the Michael Parkinson of Ulster Television. Other well-known Irish country singers include Joe Dolan, Philomena Begley and Ann Breen. But never the late presenter Hughie Green, *I seen Hughie Green once on a Butlin's holiday in Scotland and he is a very rude man. He told dirty jokes and there were ladies in the room.* Always the gentleman, where manners, please and thank you, no swearing and consideration for others, reflect the hallmark of Ray's character and personality.

Ray is as much a performing artist as many of the 'stars' that he meets. A recitalist of poetry, including some of the longest and most challenging prose from memory. A singer with a ready repertoire of ballads, songs and hymns to perform on demand or to an audience of one or more on stage. With a peculiar, selective memory recall for verse, lyrics, dates, and people, yet Ray could hardly recall a place recently visited or a meal recently eaten. To mask this memory lapse, Ray perfects a distracting method to avoid answering simple questions, such as *who did you talk to today* by responding with a clever but unrelated yet deflecting reply such as *did you know that I met Daniel O'Donnell in CastleCourt Shopping Centre and he talked with me for ages.* Asked if he went anywhere nice for his summer holidays, Ray would extend his arm and point to his suntan to simply imply somewhere nice and sunny overseas, but actually Somerset. A very clever technique for providing a reply to any question he couldn't or didn't wish to answer.

I sometimes think that autism hides our ability to see the intelligent genius that pulsates just below the surface. Scratch just deep enough and this alternative way of thinking and reasoning can be creatively astounding.

> *The only way that we can live, is if we grow. The only way that we can grow is if we change. The only way that we can change is if we learn. The only way we can learn is if we are exposed. And the only way that we can become exposed is if we throw ourselves out into the open. Do it. Throw yourself.*
>
> – C. JoyBell C.

Chapter 13

Reunited – Doe, Ray and *Me*

To the outside world, we all grow old. But not to brothers and sisters. We know each other as we always were. We know each other's hearts. We share private family jokes. We remember family feuds and secrets, family griefs and joys. We live outside the touch of time.

Clara Ortega

The clock in my head begins ticking. Softly at first, but progressively gaining momentum and volume until it dominates *Me*.

Christmas focuses upon Ray's excitement, my regressed child, substituting for my children who are now young adults. Reminiscent of Christmases past, Ray can't contain the excitement of opening his presents, traditionally after family lunch and before the Queen's speech to the Commonwealth nations at three o'clock in the afternoon. I long ago discovered that the secret of happiness for Ray lies in the quantity of presents received not the quality of gift given. The key to discovering this delightful innocence is caused by Doe who accidentally gifts a pair of socks in separate wrappings, one sock in each. Ray opens one present with a shout of excited discovery, followed by a second present prompting a comparable shout of *look, I've got another sock to match the first one.* Asking who sent the socks Ray replies, *I don't know, but they must have talked to each other to get them to match.*

January 2015 and Ray's day centre telephones *Me* to report a persistent cough. I'm not overly concerned as Ray isn't coughing at home and put this anomaly down to the air conditioning or excessive central heating within the centre. Tick.

St. Patrick's Day on 17th March always heralds the annual reopening of our caravan park for the season ahead. T packs Ray and *Me* into the car and off we go to inspect how our caravan has survived over the winter closure. Travelling through Banbridge we head towards South Down and enter the Kingdom of Mourne on the scenic but twisty route towards Castlewellan. Just short of entering Castlewellan our progress is halted by a queue of cars that are causing a static tailback for more than a mile from the town. The weather is exceptional for March with the sun 'shining on the Irish' for the succession of street parades taking place across the country. Assuming we need to just sit it out until the blockage ahead is cleared, we settle back for an uncertain waiting time. Ray seems uncharacteristically agitated and unsettled. Just the heat. His fidgeting on the front seat becomes irritating and I start to pay more attention to Ray rather than the panoramic view through the side window of the car. Sensing that Ray is building up to being sick, looking grey and sweaty, I quickly rummage through the car pockets to find a plastic bag, just managing to hold it in front of Ray's mouth as the first bout of vomiting erupts. Believing that Ray has been sitting cramped in the front seat for too long in the mid-morning sun I open his door to help him stretch his legs and to let some fresh air reach his lungs. After one or two follow-on attempts to be sick again, Ray settles a little, the cars ahead are moving and we quickly make ready to complete our journey to the coast. Tick.

By April Ray is causing *Me* greater concern. Increasingly over the preceding weeks, eating has become more difficult, both at home and at his day centre. Suspecting a throat infection, a course of antibiotics is prescribed and runs its course, but this effects little improvement. Left to his own devices, Ray eats little of any meal. My maternal instinct takes control, monitoring every meal, and I start a regime of mashing and then purifying Ray's food, spoon-feeding his breakfast and evening dinner to ensure a reasonable daily intake of calories and nutrients. Frequently the food returns almost as quickly as its spooned. This prompts *Me* to organise two visits to the GP's surgery in two weeks before I manage to secure an outpatient appointment with the Ear, Nose and Throat (ENT) department within Craigavon Area Hospital. The therapist assesses Ray's swallow and can't identify any obvious physical blockages but acknowledges that Ray appears to be experiencing physical difficulty swallowing food and most attempts at eating lead to spontaneous retching. Considering the possibility that a previous throat infection may have caused a physical difficulty and a fear of swallowing, the therapist alludes to the possibility that Ray's condition may be more psychosomatic than physical this time around. A 'simple' diagnosis offered is *a continuing fear that swallowing is difficult, leading to sickness and therefore eating is to be avoided*. A big leap of faith for *Me* as I don't believe that Ray can think it through to this extent. As a precautionary measure, the therapist promises to make a referral to the hospital for a deeper camera inspection of Ray's throat to be able to rule out any possibility of *Oesophagitis, an inflammation of the lining of the oesophagus, or the tube that carries food from the throat to the stomach*.

The therapist makes an emergency appointment for Ray but warns *Me* that this could take up to six weeks to secure a date. Tick.

The following weeks show little, if any, improvement and every day begins a stressful battle to feed Ray little and often around the clock but with frustratingly slow progress. Waiting for his 'emergency' appointment becomes intolerable. I'm reminded of the anxieties of caring for my babies when teething, trying vainly to ensure they eat when all they want to do is spit it out. Ray is my baby now. A twelve-stone man but my baby. His vulnerability and dependence upon *Me* has become absolute, and yet I feel 'absolutely' useless and impotent to help. I can't wait six weeks and make another appointment to visit Ray's GP. This time I bring T as moral support to help impress upon the doctor that I'm not simply an over-protective or overwrought sister. The consultation is going nowhere and T loses patience with the doctor, demanding to know *are you going to do nothing until he simply wastes away? This isn't right, we know something is very wrong. Is there no one left in this Health Service capable of making decisions?* Although I fully understand that T's outburst is prompted by a deep sense of mounting fear and worry, I do feel and remonstrate with him that his 'attack' against the doctor was a little unjustified.

If they can't find anything and all the tests are coming back normal it's not their fault, I reason with T to try and defuse his mounting frustration.

Sometimes you just need to shout a little louder to be properly heard and understood is T's pragmatic reply.

As reward for T's outburst, the doctor does dispatch us across town to A&E for a further assessment. The only concern identified is mild dehydration and, after a saline drip is administered, we are discharged home having waited for around five hours. Tick.

Maybe the ENT therapist is right. Maybe Ray's condition is psychosomatic and it's all in his head. With no worsening of his condition and with Ray now getting enough fluids to sink the Titanic, I begin to relax and accept continuing spoon-feeding as simply a new phase in my care for Ray. Tick.

Due to Ray's illness, we have been stonewalling an invitation for T, Ray and *Me* to attend a wedding on 22nd May in Perth, Scotland, for the son of good friends Martin and Roselyn. Having consoled ourselves that Ray is becoming more stable, a final decision is made to attend, since the trip just might lift Ray's spirits as Martin is a very special friend to Ray and he gets so much pleasure from Martin's companionship and banter. The thought of the trip seems to work and Ray is back on top form, excited about visiting Scotland and attending the wedding. The short flight over to Glasgow goes well, and Ray even manages for the first time in weeks to drink a full can of Coca-Cola. Ray stays with T and *Me* in a family room and sleeps soundly, rising early as usual and begins to enthusiastically chatter about the wedding day ahead. Having travelled by hire car up to Perth the previous evening, the onward car journey to the wedding venue to attend our first humanist wedding, *not a naturist wedding Ray*, is both short and very entertaining. Trying to explain the difference between humanist and naturist has T and *Me* in fits of laughter and lifts all our spirits. Arriving at the pre-wedding reception, Ray immediately becomes inexplicably very emotional and upset, and struggles to eat or drink without immediately vomiting. T does his best to distract Ray and minimise any disruption or focus away from the wedding. We survive the outdoor wedding ceremony and retreat to the reception area. The first floor reception room is a nightmare for access with a wheelchair, having to navigate a very steep back stairwell to reach the room with the only toilet facilities available back down the stairs and located across an adjacent courtyard. Such a wonderful wedding but such a horrendous experience for poor Ray. Tick.

A busy day on 23rd June again with *Me* taking Ray to attend the GP surgery for urine and blood tests. Ray is in good form and has a great time with *Me* visiting old friends in the afternoon. That evening Ray cannot steady his legs to rise from his seat in front of the television and T needs to physically carry Ray to his bedroom for the first time ever. Tick.

Ray's test results from the previous day all come back negative and clear of any obvious infections. Martin visits Ray and gives T and *Me* a couple of hours' respite to shop for groceries. Despite toileting Ray just before Martin's arrival, in our absence Ray asks Martin to help him to the toilet. Halfway, Ray's legs collapse again and Martin struggles to assist Ray to and from the toilet. All that effort and Ray can't pee. Martin is shocked at how much Ray's 'dead weight' can be and cannot understand how I manage Ray on my own. Tick.

Ray insists upon attending his day care centre on 25th June and the doctor telephones *Me* to say if Ray continues to be persistently sick that we *should consider taking him straight to hospital*. Tick.

I take Ray with *Me* to the GP's surgery early on the morning of Friday 26th June and the doctor gives *Me* a note to take to A&E. T drives us to hospital where Ray is provided with immediate tests. Ray's blood shows high levels of inflammation and Ray is diagnosed with pneumonia in both lungs, most acutely in his right lung and is immediately admitted onto a ward for further tests and observations. Tick.

Saturday morning, 27th June, and Ray is put on nil by mouth. A stricture is found in Ray's gullet that may explain his difficulty with swallowing and the doctors now suspect that some food or fluids may have spilled into Ray's lungs, possibly through coughing whilst trying to eat, causing the pneumonia to develop. Ray is put on an antibiotic drip and pure oxygen to assist with his breathing. During the evening Ray becomes tachycardic. T and *Me* are asked to step outside the curtains surrounding Ray's bed whilst the nursing team stabilise his condition. Tick.

The world implodes around *Me* on Wednesday 1st July. The doctor asks to speak to T and *Me* privately in the ward sister's office. *Ray is very seriously ill and he may not survive.* I can't take his words in. For months, nothing is found then suddenly, within days, Ray may die on *Me*. I don't believe it. I won't believe it. I won't let this happen to my Ray. Tick.

Doe is contacted and within 24 hours arrives at the hospital. Tick.

The following afternoon Ray is moved to the 'resuscitation' ward on the second floor and settled into a more private side room. A food bag is introduced to feed through Ray's chest, high level fluid antibiotics are dripped to his left arm, a saline solution to support rehydration dripping into his right arm and an oxygen mask is attached over his mouth and nose. Having negotiated without compromise to remain with Ray throughout while on the previous ward, I now convert his new side room into a temporary home, determined to stay until Ray gets better and is discharged back home with *Me*. No one appears to question or object to *Me* setting up residence beside Ray. Tick.

Ray appears to be rallying. The food bag is a constant companion by his side but Ray begins to ask for something to eat. The poor mite hasn't eaten real food since his admission. I try to explain to Ray that he is being fed from a special bag through his chest until we can sort out the problem with his swallowing. *But I can't taste anything,* he replies. For a distraction, T buys for Ray a new portable CD player with a large set of plug-in headphones in his favourite colour, fire-engine red. Ray chooses an old Jim Reeves gospel CD and begins to wear the tracks thin with constant replaying. To motivate Ray's recovery, I contact as many of our mutual friends that I can reach to encourage visitors who are not away on holiday as the school term has come to an end. A steady trickle becomes a flow and, although Ray greets each new visitor with a welcoming look of acknowledgement, he almost immediately reverts to listening to his old friend Jim Reeves. I strike a deal with Ray. *You're always asking for more visitors and asking who's coming to see you next, but you leave Me to do all the talking. You say 'hello' and thank each one for coming and I will do all the talking to them in between. Deal?*

Deal and he giggles.

With all the ups and downs with Ray I almost lose sight of Jay's forthcoming wedding scheduled for 18th July. Since the beginning of Ray's sickness earlier in January, T and *Me* have procrastinated about how we could be in two places at once. We can't miss our son's wedding organised to be held in the Philippines. Jay's fiancée Mariam, although Australian, is Filipino in origin and the kids chose to be married by Mariam's uncle, a Jesuit priest, in her ancestral home where many of her extended family still reside; and there is no way that we can leave Ray until we are assured of his health. In good faith, we booked the return flights in January, although we knew that Ray could not travel with us, a compromise arrived when we all received a further invitation to attend another wedding for the daughter of long-standing friends from Hillsborough; also on 18th July but closer to home in Belfast. As Doe also received an invitation to each wedding for 18th July, the solution seems almost an act of divine intervention. Doe takes Ray to the Belfast wedding allowing T and *Me* to attend our son's wedding in the Philippines.

Ray's observations are showing improvement. The inflammation in his bloods is lowering and the antibiotics appear to be clearing the infection in his lungs. For the first time, Ray can get out of bed to sit in his wheelchair and tries to eat a small pot of fortified yogurt and to drink from a glass tumbler. The oxygen mask is removed too and the grey pallor in his face is showing signs of renewed colour. New hope rises in *Me*. Ray, the comeback kid is going to recover and we're all going to a wedding. My heart begins to soar again. Tick.

As Tuesday 14th July, flight day to make the journey for the wedding in the Philippines on 18th July begins to loom large, a decision can no longer be avoided.

Monday 13th July, once again my world explodes. Ray is relapsing fast and his treatment plan is hastily restored but does not seem to be having any effect. Tick.

The most heart breaking decision I will ever be forced to make must be taken.

Ray has been in our care for almost thirty years and has but a few hours or days left; how can we miss a single minute now?

Jay has been with us for just over thirty years and God willing will be with us for the next thirty years, so surely he can forgive T and *Me* for sacrificing and missing just one day in his life; albeit a very special day, but at least with Jay we can look forward to enjoying many, many special days ahead.

T makes the heart-breaking international call to Jay. *I'm sorry son, we can't make it.*

I know Dad, Mariam and I fully understand. It's the right decision, the only decision that you and Mum could ever have made.

On 14th July Andi boards the long haul flight with a heavy heart to represent our family at our son's wedding. In her pocket, she carries T's wedding speech for Martin to deliver in his absence.

On the morning of Saturday 18th July, Jay's wedding morning, T is sitting with *Me* in the hospital canteen. I stare despairingly into T's red eyes and quietly say, as much to T as myself, *the kids are on top of the world right now and I can't help but feel that the bottom is about to fall out of ours.*

Having slept peacefully all day, on Sunday evening 19th July Ray suddenly lifts his shoulders off the bed as a torrent of blood explodes from his mouth. Twice more in the intervening hours this happens again. An undiagnosed abscess in his lung has ruptured. The bleeding is temporarily controlled by the nursing staff and Ray settles into a deeper sleep. Tick.

Much to everyone's amazement, Ray survives the night and continues to sleep peacefully through most of the night into Monday morning.

10.40am T accidentally bumps into the side of Ray's bed causing Ray to waken just long enough to ask *is it time to go to my day centre?* Tick.

T sheds a tear at the thought that, in Ray's present world, he feels safety tucked up in his own bed at home.

3.00pm Ray stirs and asks for a bottle, *I need to pee he murmurs*. Tick.

3.30pm Ray's vital organs begin to shut down. The nurse in charge administers a morphine injection to mitigate against any pain, although Ray shows no sign of discomfort and continues to sleep quietly. Tick.

T, Doe and *Me* remain gathered around Ray's bed. Little is said. Tick.

11.55pm on Monday 20th July 2015, the motion of time stops. The ticking is inaudibly and peacefully silent.

I am Me and He will forever live on through Me

Charles Raymond (Ray) Thompson
4th October 1959 – 20th July 2015

If you gave someone your heart and they died, did they take it with them? Did you spend the rest of forever with a hole inside you that couldn't be filled?

Jodi Picoult

Chapter 14

The loss in *Me*

> *And once the storm is over, you won't remember how you made it through, how you managed to survive. You won't even be sure, whether the storm is really over. But one thing is certain. When you come out of the storm, you won't be the same person who walked in. That's what this storm's all about.*
>
> Haruki Murakami

I can offer no greater testament to Ray than to share with each of you, who have faithfully travelled and shared in Ray's journey with *Me*, the words that celebrated Ray's temporary separation from our earthly lives.

In preparing our service of celebration and thanksgiving for Ray, as a family we chose to reflect upon Ray's choice of songs, hymns and poetry that brought great joy to Ray and, through Ray, to all those whose lives he touched. In the rawness of sorrow can emerge some of the greatest time for reflection and truthful insight. I offer you a small measure of this through sharing the songs, verse and spoken tributes taken from our farewell to Ray.

Entering the church, I am overwhelmed with joy and gratitude to recognise the many faces of family, friends and past and distant acquaintances that had interrupted their summer holidays to take time to support *Me* and my family in our grief and sorrow. Their presence and smiles as I entered the church for the long, lonely walk to the reserved pews to the front right, give *Me* a renewed strength to maintain my composure and dignity against the mounting eruption of emotional, yet seemingly physical pain, that threatened to tear my heart from my chest. Andi had organised for Ray's favourite song, 'My Forever Friend' recorded by Charlie Landsborough, to be played on a continuous loop choreographed to a montage of projected photographs that depicted Ray's life and many happy and memorable experiences. A selfless act of devotion created by Andi in the days and hours before that I know will have challenged her own sense of loss and grief as each captured a special moment in time and memory. In the still of the now crowded church, I too joined the hypnotic solace afforded by the images and lyrics that seemed to lift my spirit and soul to a place of indescribable peace and comfort, each line of verse and chorus guiding *Me* closer towards realising that He too is, and has always been, 'My Forever Friend'. My Friend from the beginning of time and my friend through all eternity.

    Hardly absorbing the brief opening words and prayers offered by the officiating minister, a close and trusted family friend, I am drawn back as T is invited to pay personal tribute to Ray and begins to take the few short steps to the lectern, knowing that his heart must weigh as heavy as his shoulders carrying the burden of trying to express in minutes the years of life that was our Ray. Demonstrating a composure and command of voice that masked his true emotion, T later describes feeling a serenity from a surreal presence that lifted his spirit and controlled his thoughts and words, enabling him to speak without hearing his own voice or recalling with any clarity what he said next.

On behalf of (*Me*), Doreen (Doe) and the wider family circle, thank you for taking the time to be with us today to bid farewell to Raymond. Your presence here today and the very many cards and expressions received have provided support and encouragement to our family during this difficult time.

I would like to say a special thank you to family and friends that have travelled some distance to be with us today, from Somerset, Bristol, London and from Scotland. I am also particularly pleased to welcome staff and friends from Manor Day Centre in Lurgan. Manor was Raymond's second home and you were all part of Raymond's extended family. Raymond would be delighted to see you here today.

(*Me*) has a simple picture that hangs on the wall over Raymond's bed at home. The words on this picture read:

> *Sweetheart*
> *If I could give you one thing in life*
> *I would give you the ability to see yourself through my eyes*
> *Then you would realise just how special you are.*

Raymond was a very special person. Special to his sisters Doe and (*Me*). Special to his brothers-in-law, Roger and myself. And a very special uncle to Jonathan, Andrea and Timothy. Your attendance here today also demonstrates the special place and memories that so many of you have held in your hearts too for Raymond.

I would like to share briefly just a very few of my special memories of Raymond with you today.

Raymond harboured no concept of being disabled. If anyone asked him about his health or condition, he would simply say that he was a mild summer asthmatic. In life Raymond accepted his disabilities as a natural part of who and what he was, never feeling disadvantaged or restricted and he lived his life to his full potential.

I once read a story about a young child asking her father why God made some people with a disability. The father's answer was that people with disabilities were special angels sent from heaven to teach us very special lessons. Throughout Raymond's life he was indeed a teacher.

To Doe and (*Me*), as young carers through to adult carers, each supported by their respective families, we all benefited from Raymond, our teacher. He taught us patience and humility, compassion and empathy, tolerance, respect and acceptance of all others and their differences. Raymond practised what he taught. Never angry, never complaining, never jealous of others or for what they had or could have achieved. Never demanding or selfish. Never petty or vindictive. Always mindful to say please and thank you and always content with the simplest pleasures in life, to be in the company of others.

As my wife (*Me*) has said many times over the past days, despite living with Raymond for a lifetime, I could never find fault or flaw in his character, personality or temperament. I often think how far short we, as his pupils, fell short but he never lost faith in us.

Alongside his vocation to teach, Raymond was a poet and a singer. In public or private, Raymond could always be called upon to provide a performance. His capacity to recite from memory a classical poem such as Daffodils by William Wordsworth or to sing a song from a wide repertoire of traditional Irish or Scottish ballads through to country music or sacred hymns was simply astounding. His capacity for recalling verse or song was only rivalled by his ability to pluck every notable date from history from his remarkable and amazing memory.

He was an astute businessman and negotiator. Raymond could magic a means to earn money out of thin air. If (Me) was bribing him to eat more vegetables by offering to pay him £1. Raymond would wait until she returned to the table and, still pushing peas around his plate, would look up at her with those big Labrador eyes and say Andrea says it's worth at least £5.

Raymond always seemed to ensure that he had two PAs on call. Pain in the bums he would call them. He would play his PAs, the ugly sisters as he affectionately referred to them, off against each other, being both the good cop and the bad cop. If (*Me*) told him no more 'Smarties' (sweets), he would tell Doe and she would slip him a couple more special pills.

If Doe banned him from Diet Coca-Cola, Raymond would wait until he caught (*Me*) alone and with a quivering lip tell her that Doe wasn't allowing him any more Coke. (*Me*) would immediately spring to his defence, tell him to ignore that 'old bossy boots' and give him another small glass of Coke.

Despite being a confirmed bachelor, a wife would only want to spend his money he would say, Raymond maintained two great love affairs during his life.

The first started in 1964 and never wavered. It was his love for the television soap, Coronation Street. We were delighted to have taken Raymond to the original Manchester studios and film-set this time last year (2014). The photographs of Raymond dropping into the homes of his soap idols and propped up behind the bar to pull a pint of bitter like Jack Duckworth at the Rovers Return, will be treasured forever.

His other great love was his 'bromance' with Daniel O'Donnell.

I wrote to Daniel in the early 1990s to let him know that Raymond was perhaps Daniel's biggest fan and to see if there was any possibility for Raymond to meet with him. I got a reply by return to say that he would be in Belfast the following Saturday and if we could be at the CastleCourt Shopping Centre for 11am he could meet with us. True to his word at

11am sharp, in walked Daniel and he spent twenty minutes talking with Raymond. The 'bromance' was cemented for life, although my affection for Daniel wore thin many times when I was woken at five or six o'clock in the morning to a duet from Raymond and Daniel.

Raymond was for all his life a true athlete. No challenge was too great and no obstacle too daunting. His determination to retain his independence was awe-inspiring. Many times, I watched as he battled to conquer the stairs to go to bed, Raymond always refusing to give in and to move to the ground floor. To me, it was comparable to climbing Slieve Donard (Northern Ireland's highest mountain) every night on the way to bed.

Two Saturday evenings back, I was sitting with Raymond in his hospital room and the Carl Frampton boxing match was showing on the television for the live defence of his world title. I couldn't help but see the parallel analogy. Raymond had gone into the ring many, many times during his life and always came out on top with a winning knockout. On this, his last great fight, just like Carl Frampton, Raymond was knocked to the floor in round one but immediately got back onto his feet and battled with courage and dignity right through to the final twelfth round.

I know that the great referee in the heavens will have judged this, Raymond's last great fight, a draw, to allow us to declare Raymond the undefeated champion of the world.

Time, as always in life, is against us, but I'm sure that each of you will have your own special memories of Raymond. If Raymond was to leave one legacy it would be that when you next meet someone less able than yourself, that you don't just see the wheelchair, the walking aid or the learning need. It is that you look beyond and truly get to know the person.

Do this, and I promise that you will always go away feeling blessed and enriched by the encounter.

I would like to finish with a personal tribute to 'Charlie's Angels'. To (*Me*), Doe and Andrea.

I was sitting in the car the morning before Raymond passed, reflecting on his condition with the peace of mind that 'Charlie's Angels' were all fussing around him in his hospital bed. I found a Daniel O'Donnell CD in my car that was still sealed, that in itself being very unusual. I opened the seal and put the CD into the car audio system and immediately found myself drawn time after time to the same track, a track that I had never heard before.

I believe that the lyrics from this track were destined to be found as Raymond's parting gift and words of comfort and assurance to his carers, his own personal angels on earth.

To (*Me*), Doe and Andi, from Raymond, 'You Are My Special Angel', recorded and sung by Ray's special friend, Daniel O'Donnell.

As T returned to his seat, the music and words sung by Daniel wrought special tears of peace and joy, not just from Charlie's own Angels but from many throughout the church for the promise of an eternal watchfulness.

In the reflective silence that followed, Andi followed in her Dad's footsteps to the front of the church to deliver a beautiful recital of 'Daffodils' by William Wordsworth (1815), Ray's favourite poem. Verses stunningly transcribed in calligraphy and framed to be given to *Me* by a dear friend in the days following the service.

To conclude the service of thanksgiving and celebration for the life Ray lived, the officiating Reverend offered his own following personal words of reflection:

When my wife and I came to live in Portadown, (*Me*) and T were among the first to introduce themselves as neighbours and we quickly came to realise that, in addition to their children, Jonathan and Andrea, there was someone else in their home who was a key part of their lives and who was an important member of our small community in that cul-de-sac. It was of course Raymond (Ray). He held court in his chair in their family room, took an interest in each visitor and regaled them with detailed background on his life, their family lives, the soaps and Daniel O'Donnell.

We all have memories of Raymond, but I especially remember his politeness, courtesy, his appreciation of everything that was done for him, his genuine smile and above all his contentedness with life. As he waited for his bus every morning to take him to his day centre sitting in his wheelchair, he had a wave for every neighbour who passed by and loved them to toot their car horn to him. There was an innocent brightness and tranquillity to Raymond that shone out clearly in our rushing world of materialism, busyness and self-centredness. He led a most contented and uncomplicated life.

You have all heard a moving tribute to Raymond by T. All of you who knew him could identify with so much of what T said and wholeheartedly agree that Raymond has touched the lives of us all and has shown us so much of what it is to be contented in life with the simplest of things. He also had this capacity to be forever cheerful and not to become focused on himself and his disability, which could so easily have been done. He turned conversation away from himself to others and their interests and concerns. He always asked about our children and how we were doing and what we were up to. We were delighted recently that he could attend my institution into my new parish in Enniskillen.

Any tribute to Raymond must acknowledge that he was so happy and content in life because he was lovingly cared for primarily by (*Me*) and T and their family but also Doreen (Doe) and her family to whom he travelled for annual holidays. I think we must also give thanks today for the devotion and dedicated care that Raymond received from those nearest to him, for whom he was the centre of their lives. As neighbours and friends, we were all simply astounded at the dedication of the family to Raymond and the years of sacrificial love, patience, attention and devotion that they have given to him.

Astoundingly, throughout Raymond's final illness with those weeks in hospital, he would have cause to complain and become overwhelmed by it. However, he did not, he deflected attention away from himself to others in every conversation. He maintained great dignity and grace in the face of difficult last days and hours and fought for life to the very end. He simply astonished his family and friends by the manner of his passing, thoughtful, undemanding and uncomplaining to his last breath. I know this meant so much to his close family, especially (*Me*) who never left his side.

We know how much a void there will be in their lives without Raymond and our prayer is that their hearts will gradually heal from their brokenness and they might find God's peace and new purposes in life in days to come.

So, we give thanks to Almighty God for Raymond, for all that he shared with us and all that he taught us in the manner of his living and dying. We commend him into the care and keeping of Almighty God who promises us a new heaven and a new life eternal.

With fitting appropriateness, our service concluded with the encouraging words sung congregationally 'Make me a channel of your peace' attributed to St. Francis of Assisi as a prayer of peace. Oh, how the spirit of this prayer of peace bequeathed to the world more than a century earlier touched my rending heart on this sad afternoon saying my farewell to Ray.

Chapter 15

The jigsaw puzzle that is *Me*

Though nobody can go back and make a new beginning...
Anyone can start over and make a new ending.

Chico Xavier

I end this book where I began by repeating my words:
    I had often read that your life flashes before you in the moments before death; like a final audit giving account for the life lived and the lessons learned. Just as suddenly as the thought enters my head, I become immersed beneath a tsunami of memories and emotions. Never-ending waves of past experiences wash over *Me*. Each memory rolling over *Me* to be succeeded by the next, and another, for a life replayed, for a life relived.
    Ray was beyond a brother to *Me*. In life, I became his guardian. In death, I trust and believe that *He* now becomes my continuing guardian amongst the many angels that touch my life.
    Our bond in life was so close that I believe in the dying moments before departing, I became the vessel for his reflective journey through this life. His story is my story. His life was my life.

I cannot explain my lucidness for retelling our life together other than as one shared journey. My thoughts are his thoughts. His pain is my pain. My joy his joy. His suffering my suffering. His laughter my laughter. We are so entwined as to be indistinguishable one from the other.

Just as in life I was, on very many occasions, Ray's voice. So too in the moments before death I became his voice for a life replayed, for a life relived.

My life has been blessed beyond measure by knowing Ray, caring for Ray, loving Ray. Loving him as my brother and in his later years as my other 'child'. His loss to *Me* is profound, as any mother who has experienced the loss of a child. And yet, amid this grief, I feel uplifted by an abiding sense of peace and joy beyond measure.

I believe we choose the life we live. Not just in the decisions and choices that we make as we travel through this adventurous journey of life, but in the choice afforded to each of us to be who we wish to be, even before we are born. If we are here to learn, to grow spiritually, to aspire to be closer to our Creator through a greater eternity, then surely we must choose the body, the family, the environment, the person we want and need to become. Only in so doing can we fully reflect the journey that we need to undertake if we are to truly strive to learn the lessons that we must learn to grow spiritually. An experiential journey towards fulfilment and a greater eternal life beyond this life.

This being so gives *Me* the greatest comfort, knowing that Ray too chose the life he desired to live.

He chose his life and to live it with *Me*. He chose his disabilities as the vehicle for his own self-learning and development and as the means to help teach those around him, if they but choose for themselves to truly look, see and understand this gift from God.

I know my perspective may be challenged by many. It may even cause offence to those who seek and choose to cross my path simply to be offended. I offer no personal offence. I mean simply to voice aloud for *Me*, for my own personal understanding, for my continuing journey, now alone, for I am no longer guided by the physical presence of my teacher. But surely this too is a part of the plan for my own continuing spiritual development.

As I continue my journey through this life I feel happy in the assurance that death is but a thin veil that separates us from those who have departed a little ahead of us. In the scale of eternal time, those who departed before will count in milliseconds the time apart, before with surety we all meet again.

To Ray, my brother, my companion, my teacher and my eternal soul mate, 'till we meet again'.

Epilogue

In this memoir of *Me* and my siblings' journey through life, together as children, separated as teenagers and reunited as adults, is a story of reflective questioning and spiritual enlightenment born in the moments before a veil of death cast its dark shadow over the departing soul of my brother Ray.

For *Me* to conclude that the life we live is the life that we choose to live, why then do we choose to suffer emotional and, in some instances, physical pain or distress?

Why do some people choose hardship over comfort?

Is the prize of continuing eternal progression a wealth greater than all the financial security or material possessions that this earthly life can provide?

For *Me*, the quest is not about seeking answers for the meaning of life, but rather the meaning and purpose of individual lives. The answer for *Me* is discovered in this personal journey of reflection that is my life relived, but recalled in and through the life of my beloved brother, Ray.

For *Me* to only fully realise that the eternal secret, the true purpose and value of the lives that we lead, in the dying moments of a life may seem a tragic irony. Rather than feeling robbed or cheated, for *Me*, the most wonderful departing gift from Ray is the belief that the life that Ray chose for himself, reveals the key to unlocking the experiences of life for *Me* too.

Just as the pathways that Doe, Ray and *Me* each chose for ourselves were inextricably linked in life, so too are they irrevocably entwined in death.

The fulfilment of each life lived as it was chosen to be lived, and expressed by the decisions and actions that we each choose therein, illuminates the gateway to our own eternities.

As one achieved adventure ends in this lifetime, so then are we elevated to the beginning of a new and even greater eternal adventure.

To God be the glory.